Gordon H. Clark
Personal Recollections

John W. Robbins
Editor

The Trinity Foundation
Jefferson, Maryland

Cover:

Gordon Haddon Clark as a young college instructor,
c. 1939

Courtesy: Lois Zeller

Gordon Haddon Clark: Personal Recollections
Copyright 1989
The Trinity Foundation
Post Office Box 169
Jefferson, Maryland 21755
Printed in the United States of America.

ISBN 0-940931-27-3

GORDON H. CLARK: PERSONAL RECOLLECTIONS

Books by John W. Robbins

Answer to Ayn Rand (1974)
The Case Against Indexation (1976)
Scripture Twisting in the Seminaries, Part 1: Feminism
    (1985)
Cornelius Van Til: The Man and the Myth (1986)
Education, Christianity, and the State (Editor, 1987)
Pat Robertson: A Warning to America (1988)

Contents

Foreword

Several years ago I decided to write a biography of Gordon Clark. When I mentioned my intention to Clark himself, he was adamantly opposed: No one, he insisted, would be interested in his life; he had done nothing exciting; he had neither led armies nor conquered kingdoms, nor discovered a cure for cancer. Who would possibly be interested in the dull life of a philosophy professor?

It was only after enlisting the aid of his family and a good deal of arm-twisting and cajoling that Clark finally agreed to help with his biography. He consented to some tape recorded interviews, turned over some papers, and he and his family made suggestions of other sources for information about his early life in Philadelphia.

I have been accumulating the information for years, but this is not Clark's biography. That book still waits to be written, and demand for it will grow as Clark's books become more and more widely read. This present book is a series of essays by those who knew Clark, essays that I solicited in anticipation of deaths among those who had known Clark for much of his life. (One of the contributors to this volume has since died.) I thought it would be best to let them tell their stories in their own words.

The contributors range in age from those in their

twenties to those who have passed three score and ten. Some are family members (Elizabeth George, Lois Zeller, Wyatt George, and Dwight Zeller); some are students (Sharon Ritchey Gingrich, Samuel Zinaich, Jr., John W. Sanderson, Carl F.H. Henry, Mary Crumpacker, Deborah Kozlowski); others are colleagues and leaders in their own fields (Ronald Nash, Roland G. Usher, Jr., J.C. Keister, Edmund P. Clowney, Ruth Bell Graham, Janet Glenn Gray, Harold Lindsell, Joseph Pattison, Robert K. Rudolph, and William Young); and one, Anna Marie Hafer, was a childhood friend. Each brings different recollections about Gordon Clark to this book, and thereby enriches us all.

This book, I should point out, is not finished. It is likely that there is someone else who knew Clark well who ought to write his recollections of the man. Should any reader who was an acquaintance of Clark wish to contribute to a second edition, please inform the editor. Not only will such additional essays fill out our understanding of Clark, but when the time comes to write a biography, there will be far more information available about a man who marshalled arguments, conquered minds, and lived the exciting life of a Christian in a fallen world.

John W. Robbins
March 4, 1989

The Witness

Edmund P. Clowney*

There was a summer day when I was digging dande-
lions on the Clark lawn (in Wheaton, Illinois). Gordon
always had a job when a student was broke. Gordon sat in a
lawn chair with a book. Along came a Jehovah's Witness
with a phonograph—much used in those days. (Judge
Rutherford was featured on the disk.) I moved behind a
bush to catch the encounter. Gordon was asking, "But what
do you believe about Jesus Christ? Is he God?" The reply
was a bit of hedging. Christ was over creation. Gordon
referred to the first chapter of John's Gospel. The Jehovah
Witness brightened—"Oh, yes, but in *Greek* it does not say
the God; the word for 'God' does not have the definite
article in John 1:1."

Gordon: "So you have studied the Greek language?"

Jehovah's Witness: "Oh, yes. We are well prepared in
the Scriptures."

Gordon then handed him the book he was reading.
"Would you mind reading this for me?" The book was
Plotinus in Greek. Gordon had been reading it without
benefit of dictionary. (I believe he prepared a concordance
to Plotinus.)

The Jehovah's Witness stared at the book, picked up
his phonograph and beat a fast retreat.

*Former president of Westminster Seminary

The Early Butler Years

Mary Crumpacker*

I first met Gordon Haddon Clark in the fall of 1945 when I returned to college to complete my undergraduate work. I have decided to focus on Clark's early Butler years, because many may not be aware of the qualities he manifested in steering one unbeliever through the pitfalls of humanism and false theology. Some of these qualities were sensitivity, tact, restraint, humility, patience, and humor. I hope to help the reader appreciate the man as I did.

To meet a social science requirement I decided to examine philosophy and enrolled in the only course that would fit my schedule—Kant. Poor Dr. Clark! Most of the students lacked the necessary prerequisites. When none of us took his suggestion to drop the course, he reluctantly continued. Reading the *Critique of Pure Reason* with beginners was a painful experience for both professor and students. For about two weeks I was lost. Then it dawned on me that in attempting to describe the limits of human knowledge, Kant was engaged in a pursuit of immense personal concern to me. If Kant could prove that the knowledge of God's existence was beyond human reason, I

*Former professor of French, Valparaiso University, Valparaiso, Indiana.

would not have to worry about what might happen after death. Surely God, if He existed, would not hold me responsible for what I could not know.

Once I realized how vitally important Kant's undertaking was to me personally, I did everything I could to make sense of him. My enthusiasm must have been an encouragement to Clark, who soon asked if I would like to grade papers, with a promise to supply all the answers. What an opportunity to gain some of the advantages of courses I would not be able to work into my schedule and to be paid for it! I am certain Dr. Clark would have welcomed class discussion, but I was too ashamed of my stupidity and ignorance to ask questions. It was that same pride and timidity that kept me from getting all I could have out of the courses I did take, for Clark was at his best when he engaged a student in an argument. All of the students would perk up and take sides and the guinea pig would invariably learn the most. Lack of confidence kept me from joining in this valuable exercise. For months I succeeded in avoiding any prolonged discussion, until one day, the second semester, I was so sure the professor would agree with me that I ventured a criticism of Leibniz' theory of pre-established harmony. Before I knew it I found myself involved in a series of questions and answers which left me humiliated and hurt—humiliated because I looked ridiculous in front of the class and hurt because I had thought Clark liked me. My reaction could not have been more childish, but my reflections on this event proved to be a crucial turning point in my pilgrimage toward Biblical faith. I concluded that Clark was probably one of those old-fashioned believers—a Calvinist perhaps—who really thought the Bible was true. To one who had no idea that a person could be a scholar and a Christian at the same time, this came as a profound shock. I think I might have dropped the course except that Dr. Clark had already won my deepest respect. I decided that if he really were a Christian, Christianity must make more sense than I had originally supposed. Because of my pride I did not ask him what he thought about God but spent the summer trying to figure out where he stood and to discover the answer to a seemingly insurmountable obstacle to the Christian faith —the problem of free will and predestination.

About the same time as my debate with Clark and its humiliating consequences, the full import of the Kant course began to sink in. Kant's effort was in vain. One cannot know the limits of human knowledge. To know that much is to know a great deal about the unknowable. Clearly this was a contradiction. When I saw Clark the following fall, I told him I thought I had the answer to the problem of free will and predestination. What presumption! Instead of laughing or frowning when I said Spinoza was right to maintain that we choose but could not have chosen otherwise, he replied politely and with the utmost seriousness: "You are making progress. Are you sure you are not neglecting responsibility?" And then, almost in the same breath. "Do you have a Bible?" Hearing an affirmative answer, he wrote down two references for me— Romans 8 and 9 and Ephesians. Obviously Paul believed in predestination. But did Jesus, I wondered, recalling something another professor had said about Paul being the trouble with Christianity? I would read the Gospels and show Clark the basic contradiction at the heart of Christianity. Needless to say, the idea of a predetermined plan jumped out at me on every page. Before finishing John, I knew the Bible was true and that I was headed for hell. I saw what a fool I had been to think I could demand the answer to every question before I examined for myself the centuries-old claims of Christ. I begged God for forgiveness for all my sins and especially for my pride and presumption.

Shortly before my conversion Clark had lent me Carl F.H. Henry's *Remaking the Modern Mind*. When I told Clark I found the book interesting, he suggested I call Dr. Henry some time when I was in the Chicago area and tell him so. No doubt Clark hoped that Henry would get me to talk where he could not seem to; but Henry was out of town. This book was one of the steps in my pilgrimage as were all the philosophy classes and paper grading, but, most of all, I would credit the lectures on medieval philosophy for removing the stumbling blocks which had closed my mind to the possibility that Christianity could be true. Clark's translation of a chapter from Etienne Gilson's *Introduction à l'Etude de Saint Augustine* proved especially helpful.

After my conversion I began looking for a church and reading the *Institutes*. Next I asked Clark how I could serve the Lord. His answer was "Study. Are you interested in exegesis, commentary, textual criticism, systematic or biblical theology, apologetics or what?" I scarcely knew what he was talking about. He invited me into his study and, there, to my chagrin, I discovered that he was a theologian as well as a philosopher and remembered his kindness when I thought I knew the answer to such problems as free will and predestination. He decided to lend me the books he thought would be the most helpful to me. Some of these were: Oswald T. Allis, *The Five Books of Moses* and *Prophecy and the Church*; A.B. Bruce, *The Humiliation of Christ*; Charles Hodge, *Romans* and *II Corinthians*; John Laidlaw, *The Bible Doctrine of Man*; Gresham Machen, *Christianity and Liberalism*, *The Origin of Paul's Religion*, *The Virgin Birth*, and *What Is*

Faith; James Orr, *A Christian View of God and the World;* William T. Shedd, *Romans,* two books on textual criticism, one by Kenyon; Gerhaardus Vos' *The Self-Disclosure of Jesus* and unpublished lecture notes on Biblical Theology; some of B.B. Warfield; and t o of his father's books, *The Message from Patmos* and *Systematic Theology.* He also recommended John Bunyan's *A Pilgrim's Progress* and C.S. Lewis' *Screwtape Letters* and *Miracles.*

In the margins of each book Clark had written careful outlines in his own neat shorthand. There was no hint as to where he agreed or disagreed with the author. Clark's procedure tells a great deal about his methodology. He evidently considered it the reader's first duty to make sure he understood what the writer was trying to say, and it was obvious that he was very careful in this regard. No wonder he was so exasperated with those colleagues who did not extend this courtesy to him!

After I was well along in my reading Clark suggested I try writing illustrations of Christian doctrines. He offered to help me and saw to it that my efforts were published. Next he thought I might try an article on literature from the Christian point of view. I was crushed when my essay on "The Presuppositions of André Gide" was turned down by *PMLA.* Actually, as I discovered on rereading it years later, the critics were more than kind. There was no criticism of the title, the organization, the Christian critique, or any of the parts where Clark had made suggestions. Only the part about Gide was at fault. I simply did not know my subject well enough, and Clark had not read Gide. I have always regretted my lack of perseverance in this regard, especially when I think of how generous Clark had been with his time. But then Professor Clark was exceedingly generous with his time with anyone who was sincerely engaged in using his talents for the Lord—especially when those gifts were ones he felt equipped to encourage.

Everyone I know who was influenced by Dr. Clark seems to have been strongly motivated by his example to develop and use his talents to the glory of God—family, friends, and students. I owe him a great deal for having encouraged me to do things I never would have tried on my own, such as teaching Sunday School and playing the organ. The organ was especially difficult for me. When he saw that I followed the congregation instead of leading it and that the singing began to drag more and more, he and his family sat up near the front where he could take the lead with his strong bass. The singing improved greatly, and I was encouraged. Whenever he could Clark taught by deeds rather than words. On another occasion, when I was trying too hard to live the Christian life and was probably exhibiting a most unattractive and pietistic legalism, he and his wife took time from their busy schedules to invite me to a movie matinee.

Clark was the most consistent Christian I have ever known. He loved the truth and seldom hesitated to express it even when silence was an option. When I asked his wife why her husband seemed to go out of his way to alienate people, she said he thought the brightest students admired professors who spoke the truth with boldness and conviction. An episode Ruth Bell Graham relates in a book entitled *It's My Turn* bears this out. One time, when her faith was being assailed by doubts, a brilliant student she had been dating suggested a visit to a particularly warm-hearted and deeply spiritual professor who had been a help to him. " 'No,' she replied. 'He will talk with me and pray with me and it could get a little emotional. I don't want that. All I want are the cold, hard facts. I wanted to go see Dr.

Clark. Clark, known for his logic, his unemotional brilliance, I felt, would give me nothing but the cold, hard facts."

One of the highlights of my Butler years was the Great Books Discussions my husband and I sometimes attended. Clark was a superb leader. Once, a visiting co-leader, a noted astronomer, chose to ignore the agreed-upon procedures and not only called attention to his own world view but tried to discredit Clark's. Clark's tongue-in-cheek manner of dealing with this situation was amusing to all but the astronomer. Turning to the astronomer, Clark asked: "How do you define space, Mr._____?" It seems that he, an expert on space, had never given the matter a thought. He must have felt as ridiculous as I did when I got my come-uppance for deriding Leibniz. In neither case did Clark give his own opinion. He let the class and the groups draw their own conclusions.

One last way in which Clark demonstrated his faith by his works was in his silence concerning his many disappointments. For example, whatever I learned of the Wheaton affair, the Van Til controversy, etc. came later and through other people. His wife had said he took very seriously Christ's warning that on the day of judgment we shall all give an account for every idle word we have spoken.

The Clarks remained very dear friends even though we ceased to see much of them after we left Indianapolis in 1951. God used Gordon Clark more than any other human instrument to draw me to Him, and I shall be eternally grateful. After giving my testimony on joining a church, an elder, who was also a college professor, remarked: "How wisely your professor handled you!" I was pleased that he understood.

Life With Father, Part I

Elizabeth Clark George

"What was it like—living in the home of Gordon Clark?"

This question has been posed to me many times, and I used to answer, "Oh, ordinary, I guess, like any other family." And indeed, it did seem to be the ordinary home life of a typical American family—until, as an adult and parent myself, I discovered it wasn't! Perhaps our home should have been likened to a Trappist monastery, for silence was the rule rather than the exception. Some would call it dull, for daily events were predictable; without doubt, it was a life of stability. But closer to what could have been Clark's own description—since he defines "person" as "a set of propositions"—it was living with four sets of propositions: Mother, Father, sister Lois, and myself.

Mother's propositions were good: "My highest priority is tender care of my family; faithful work in the church is an expression of love; schoolteaching must be done competently, to God's glory." Lois's propositions were admirable: "Diligence and organization are important; music and younger sister are to be loved." My proposition was single: "Today I play." My father's proposition was also single: "Thy Word is truth." Upon that proposition and its corollary, "I will obey Thy Word," the life of Gordon Clark was founded. Based on examples of his obedience to several of God's commands, I offer you a glimpse into Clark's personal life.

Redeeming the Time

The problem of time and eternity is perplexing. Somehow it seems that the "eternal present" of God is easier to grasp than time's future fleeting into past. Yet God has given us "times and seasons" and has commanded us to "walk circumspectly, not as fools, but as wise, redeeming the time, because the days are evil." Gordon Clark certainly endeavored to put this into practice; scarcely a wasted moment can be charged to his account. This is not to say that he was an action-packed whirlwind; on the contrary, he was deliberate, almost slow in his activities. However, his choice of activities was purposeful and carried to completion with a steadiness of daily schedule that was impressive.

Each day in the Clark home began with a very plain breakfast, after which the quiet husband either said simply, "Thank you, Ruthie," and disappeared, or got out the Bible, read a chapter, and asked my sister and me a question or two of the Shorter Catechism. By the time I had finished high school, we had covered the catechism fairly thoroughly, for which I have always been grateful.

On the normal Monday-Wednesday-Friday school day, Clark, a philosophy professor at Butler University, was gone from 7:30 to 12:30. On Tuesdays, Thursdays, Saturdays, and summer days, he studied for an uninterrupted five hours. If we children were at home, we certainly had to be quiet, and lunchtime was a welcome break! After lunch came naptime for the thinker; again it was essential for everyone to be quiet! By mid-afternoon, two or three times a week, the chess colleague, Robert Andry, arrived, complete with cigar; silence (and smoke) reigned again for two hours or so, ending simply with the "Checkmate," a warm handshake, and two contented smiles. After 600 such games, not counting the draws, Andry claimed 298 victories; Clark had 302. They were a marvelous pair. (These two also enjoyed the local chess club, in which each claimed championships at one time or another, and I am now personally happy to have the championship plaque presented to Clark by the "King's Men Chess Club" in 1966.)

Afternoon and evening routines were, of course, broken more frequently than in the morning. There were occasional activities connected with Butler University; he loved the receptions given by the Home Economics Department! Evenings often saw church work, speaking engagements, Great Books Club, Alliance Française meetings, the well-loved King's Men Chess Club, oil painting classes, watercolor classes, or guests in the home. It was always pleasant to have guests; Mother would make dinner, the table was beautifully set, and conversation was easy and agreeable. On such occasions the usually silent head of the house could be quite a conversationalist. Some of our favorite guests were five or six single ladies or widows in our church who were absolutely delightful people. There was also a German family whose serious countenances belied the quick-witted and humorous interchange that sparked the evening and fascinated us completely. And without doubt, one of our privileges was the frequent reception of missionaries and other Christian passers-by. Such evenings entailed serious spiritual discussion, for the days are evil, and the time must be redeemed.

The normal evening routine, however, was a quiet meal in the breakfast nook of the kitchen, followed by a daily walk—usually father, daughter, and dog. Then came three more hours of solid concentration. It was during these evenings that I remember peeking into the study and seeing my father reading, writing, and often praying. Each evening he sat on the same chair, at the same desk, with the same Greek Bible, Greek Lexicon, and King James Bible open before him. His Bible went all through life with him, and inside the front cover is written, "Gordon H. Clark, given to me by my mother, c. 1912-13? rebound, Feb. 1938." There is scarcely a mark in the entire volume, but the pages are ragged and dirty, and the 1938 binding has collapsed. I think its owner figured that he would meet its Author before another binding became obligatory. The temporal passes away; the eternal endures forever.

In daily life, the routine ended with prayer; and God grants sleep to those whom he loves. And so the philosopher retired about 10:30 p.m., anticipating a fresh awakening at 5:30 or 6:00, with perhaps an hour of study to look forward to before breakfast. Redeem the time!

Fathers, Love Your Children
The Word of God exhorts fathers to love their children. This is a gracious command that our father did not appear to find difficult to obey. His day by day gentleness and interest in our activities demonstrated his love. When he was away from home, he wrote us letters. When he returned, there were barrettes or a ring for a little girl; sheet music or a make-up kit for a teen; a lovely pin for his wife. Tangible and intangible, his love was evident.

One thing I regret is that he did not freely discuss with us his thinking and writing. As I grew older and became more interested in his thought, I would occasionally ask him about a variety of topics. His standard response was that I could find pertinent information in a book; he usually gave me the author and volume, and sometimes even the page number. But, love or no love, he expected me to ferret out whatever information I wanted, just like any other student.

Occasionally, on our evening walks, I could pry some bits of scholarship out of him, but it was rare. He was more interested in talking about the sky, the stars, and infinity, or perhaps describing Philadelphia in 1910. Those were the days when John Philip Sousa's band played at the Willow Grove park, and the concerts were outstanding. Those were the days, too, when my great-grandfather was alive, and he was probably the person—other than Paul, Augustine, and Calvin—whom my father respected most. His name was Thomas Deacon Haddon, born in England in 1834, and by profession a wool carder. Why did the philosopher, to the end of his life, so respect the simple wool carder? Because as a child he saw his elderly grandfather study and master Greek, in order better to understand the Word of God. This is love.

Love can be demonstrated in many ways. Part of loving a child includes putting up with peculiarities and embarrassing situations. I wonder how many times I embarrassed my father; dare I recount one potentially awkward event? I loved animals, and always had birds, turtles, fish, chameleons—whatever my parents would permit. One sad day, my turtle, Racer, died. I was always very upset when my pets died, and I had a wonderful little cemetery by the garage where the trees were tall and the bushes formed a hideaway. I prepared the coffin for Racer and dug the grave. Then it occurred to me how nice it would be to have a "guest minister" perform the funeral service. And who happened to be visiting us at the time but Dr. William Young, a philosophy professor (currently at Providence-Barrington College)! I do not recall that either Dr. Young or my father even so much as hinted at the oddity of the situation; both calmly came out to pay their last respects to Racer, and Dr. Young gave a beautiful funeral message and prayer. It was without doubt the best funeral that any of our pets ever had, and I will be forever grateful to Dr. Young; he certainly proved his friendship and his magnanimity by that act of genuine kindness, greatly appreciated by a little girl. Her father understood completely.

Another evidence of the thoughtful care of the family was the pleasant trips we had. Sometimes there was a one-day excursion to a State Park, and more memorable were the long summer vacations, eventually covering nearly every corner of the country. Most outstanding was our 1954 trip to Europe, a four-month discovery of the wonders of the Old World. Not that we rushed from place to place; quite the opposite—it was a slow-paced, relaxed tour. We spent nearly a month in Paris, beginning each day with a leisurely "petit déjeuner" in the café next to the hotel, and visiting only one place each day—a museum, a park, a chateau, a cathedral—stopping for tea in the afternoon, and strolling through the Jardin du Luxembourg in the evening to the restaurant in the Student Quarter where my parents had eaten when they were students in 1929. (I was later to return to that same restaurant in 1960 and in 1965, but by 1982 it was closed to the public and had become a student-only cafeteria. During off-hours, I ventured in and found the cook, who, when I told him that my parents had eaten there in 1929, offered to get me a pass from the student service of the Sorbonne. I declined, but wish now that I had accepted his offer!) But, back to 1954—the leisurely discovery of Paris, plus a week each in Luzerne, Heidelberg, Amsterdam, and Edinburgh fixed those cities forever in my mind. The final month was in London, from which my mother, sister, and I branched out a bit. We had had our fill of art museums, though the philosopher had not, so we left him in the good company of Victoria and Albert, while we spent a delightful day in Canterbury, and another unforgettable day at Stonehenge. That was in the era when very few people visited Stonehenge—it was a two-mile hike from Amesbury—and the field was a wide-open cow pasture. I remember my indescribable awe as I moved from stone to stone, touching, measuring, imagining, wondering. . . . Let him who will enjoy interminable rooms of paintings; I have a fascination for stone circles! No matter . . . the loving father had opened a world of delight for his daughters. He loved us.

Support the Weak

Many people found Gordon Clark to be a hard man: cold, ruthless, blunt, unsympathetic, disdainful. I never heard him castigate anyone or any group as a "generation of vipers" (he left that to the One who knows all), but he was indeed rather unsympathetic to people who were quite intelligent but whose thinking was inconsistent, or to those who were not intelligent but had the definite opinion that they were. Perhaps he should have been more patient with such people. But his interpretation of the Biblical injunction to "support the weak" was to take the time to help those whom he saw as truly "weak." I remember with pleasure and some amusement my father's attempts to teach a certain teenage boy to read. This boy had attended our Sunday School for several years, and by the time he reached eighth grade he still could barely read. My father patiently worked with him one afternoon a week after school for quite a long time. I am not sure that the reading results were successful, but young Roger certainly enjoyed the many hours with his "good buddy Dr. Clark"!

Another person to whom Clark gave his attention and care was a very intelligent black girl, Jimi Davis. She had endeared herself to him, and he was saddened when she was struck with tuberculosis. Over a period of many months he made frequent trips to the sanitorium to visit with Jimi and to encourage her on her long road to recovery.

There were other hospital calls, nursing home visits, and trips to visit people in prison. There were trips to the farm of an elderly man and his sister who needed some special care. In later years, living near Chattanooga, he enjoyed helping a group of Cambodians learn to read and speak English. For, in spite of what appeared to be an outer coldness, Clark did sincerely care for the weak.

Preach the Word

My earliest recollections of my father's preaching go back to the late 1940's and early 50's when we were attending a United Presbyterian Church in Indianapolis. The congregation had a pastor, so Clark preached there only as a substitute, but there were other United Presbyterian churches in central Indiana that were without pastors from time to time. He would preach for those congregations, often for many months, and on occasion I accompanied him. Thus it was that I became acquainted with the churches in Rushville, Bloomington, Salem, and other small towns which I now look back on with a fading but pleasant memory. In 1957, the pastor of the Indianapolis church died, and it was natural that Clark should become the pulpit supply. 1957 and 1958 were tedious years as the United Presbyterian Church was in the midst of deciding whether to merge with the Presbyterian Church, USA, the denomination we had left in 1936 with Dr. Machen. When the merger was accepted, the Indianapolis church, under Clark's leadership, withdrew from the denomination and joined the Reformed Presbyterian Church, General Synod. There followed a court battle over the church property which became a long, drawn-out affair. The little congregation—it numbered only about 25-30 souls—had a quitclaim from the nineteenth century which was upheld by some courts but rejected by others, and in the end the property was lost. Thanks to the faithful commitment of several people, the small congregation managed to construct a new building, and with the Lord's blessing over the years, the group has grown to the strong body that it is today. That growth did not come during the time Clark preached there, but he had made it possible by serving the church for eight of the most tenuous years of its existence.

I know there were other speaking and preaching engagements in a variety of places, but perhaps the most interesting and and unusual was the "Good News Mission," a little building in downtown Indianapolis across the street from the train station. In the 1980's the station has become a fancy shopping and restaurant complex; a few decades ago, it was a busy but dirty building, surrounded by bars, cheap hotels, vacant buildings, and fortune tellers' shops, from whose dimly-lit recesses emerged innumerable gypsy children. In the midst of the city squalor, lit up by a cross at night, was the "Good News Mission." Inside, hot meals and clean beds were offered to anyone who would come to the evening service. They may have been so drunk they didn't know the front of the room from the back, but if they sat there, they got their meal. And many nights, over a period of probably twenty years, sitting there meant being preached at by a philosophy professor who knew how to open the gospel to the destitute. Long years ago in England, a preacher was criticized for preaching about sin when he addressed the House of Lords, but he replied that they knew nothing of sin, whereas at Newgate Prison he preached forgiveness because the prisoners already knew they were sinners in need of grace. In similar manner, I have heard Clark deliver messages of sin that shocked the educational elite, while at the city mission he offered mercy and grace to help the wanderers in their time of need.

Out of the Abundance of the Heart, His Mouth Speaketh

The aggravatingly careless use of the terms "heart" and "head" which are tossed about in Christian conversation today ought to be constantly challenged until Christians realize that by disparaging the "head" they are actually denouncing the "heart" with which one is able to *think*. The "heart" is not superior to the mind, placing faith above understanding; the heart *is* the mind, and faith *is* understanding. With a mind renewed by the Holy Spirit, one can believe on the Lord Jesus Christ and be saved. With the heart one meditates, understands sin, repents, confesses, receives forgiveness, strives to make his calling and election sure, loves the Lord, walks in his way, serves faithfully, and endures to the end. The mind is not dry, dull, and spiritually detached; nor does the heart produce some emotional frill that supposedly substantiates salvation.

The head and the heart are synonyms, regenerate in some people, unregenerate in others. And out of the abundance thereof, the mouth speaketh.

Gordon Clark spoke what was in his heart. He said unequivocally, "I know whom I have believed, and am persuaded . . . ." His many books testify to his faith. Yet, sadly, even almost to the end of his life, there were those who were skeptical of his salvation. All "head," no "heart"? On the contrary, all head, all heart. His affirmation of grace was clear, consistent, and firm to the end. But some people are more persuaded by tears, and perhaps it is good to know that Clark also shed tears, both publicly and privately—usually over his inability to keep the first and greatest commandment, which failure sent Christ to the cross. But tears express little unless one knows the words behind them. And so I gladly share with you some words spoken out of the abundance of his heart:

> Thus far did I come, laden with my sin.
> Nor could aught ease the grief that I was in,
> Till I came hither. What a place is this!
> Must here be the start of all my bliss?
> Must here, the burden fall from off my back?
> Must here, the strings that bound it to me, crack?
> Blest cross! blest sepulchre! blest, rather, be
> The Man that there was put to shame for me.

Who is a Rock, Save our God?

There are certain places on the face of the earth that could be considered favorites of Gordon Clark: Shiprock, Half Dome, Monument Valley, the Black Canyon of the Gunnison, Boquillas Canyon. He visited these places in the summers, and did oil paintings of them at home in the winters. He often commented on their massive and majestic beauty, and agonized that the colors he mixed on the canvas never equalled the real thing.

In the summer of 1984, it was my privilege to take my father on a trip. We decided to visit Santa Fe, Albuquerque, White Sands, El Paso,—and Big Bend National Park. My parents had had a wonderful trip there several years earlier, and it had been my father's desire to return. Boquillas Canyon was our planned destination. Leaving the car in the parking lot we began the hike—and what a hike! It was August, and August in southern Texas affords no breeze or relief from the blazing sun. Two of my boys were with us and of course they ran ahead; Clark, aged 82, and I, feeling like 82, trudged along behind. Nonetheless, we made it, and found the effort rewarded; the Canyon was beautiful. And I must say, after that grueling hike, I had increased respect for the stamina of my octogenarian father!

There is one rock that I wish Clark could have visited, not for its beauty, for in itself it is not so very impressive, but for the history (actual or traditional) that transpired there. It is the famous cleft in the cliff where Augustus Toplady took shelter during a storm and wrote the hymn *Rock of Ages*. Since it expresses so beautifully Clark's own testimony, and since as his favorite we sang it so often, it is only fitting that I conclude my recollections of my father with its truly moving words:

Rock of Ages, cleft for me, let me hide myself in Thee;
Let the water, and the blood, from Thy riven side which flowed,
Be of sin the double cure. Cleanse me from its guilt and power.

Not the labors of my hands could fulfill Thy law's demands.

Could my zeal no respite know, could my tears forever
flow—
All for sin could not atone. Thou must save, and Thou
alone.

Nothing in my hand I bring; simply to Thy cross I cling.
Naked, come to Thee for dress. Helpless, look to Thee for
grace.
Foul, I to the fountain fly. Wash me, Saviour, or I die.

While I draw this fleeting breath, when my eyelids close in
death,
When I soar to worlds unknown, see Thee on Thy judgment
throne—
Rock of Ages, cleft for me, let me hide myself in Thee.

Memories of a Father-in-Law

Wyatt George

There are a few memories that I think are interesting and helpful to an understanding of Dad Clark. These memories are colorful and often fascinating. They stretch over a period of eighteen years, and, since his death, continue to be a lively source of laughter as we relay them to our children.

My earliest, most vivid memory of him was when I asked for his daughter's hand in marriage. I seized upon the evening routine of walking the dog as an opportune time to broach the question. We began our walk, talking about the neighborhood as he introduced the dogs from house to house! First there was Susie, next door. Next, Skipper. Then Cinnamon. As we passed a house with no dog, I decided to get straight to my point, realizing he would appreciate a direct approach. "Dr. Clark," I began, "the reason I came here this week-end was to ask if I could marry your daughter. May I have your permission to marry Betsy?" His surprising answer came without the slightest hesitation (though I had been dreading the awkwardness of a silent pause), "Oh, Betsy is over 21. She can do whatever she wants to do. Now, in these next two houses live Rex and Angel . . . ."

27

Later, when Betsy and I had our own home, Dad Clark frequently came to visit. Often, he would just sit and read, usually a volume totally unrelated to his life as a philosopher, but which illuminated his teaching. His sermons and arguments in private conversation were always peppered with observations that came from his extraneous readings, his travels, or his conversations with neighbors. Often his frustrations with regular life gave him occasions to illustrate.

Once, after some automobile problems, which he tended with considerable groaning, he and I were at the dining room table discussing predestination. His part in the dialogue was as matter of fact as Thanksgiving turkey. Sensing a little smugness in his beliefs and understanding, I asked if he had any problems at all with predestination. His answer, so uncharacteristic that it totally astonished me and ended the conversation, was that he did not know of any doctrine that did not present a problem to him.

Perhaps the confidence he had in the Lord and in the doctrines of grace were what we needed to hear at all times, for why should he bother us with what he had not yet figured out? In reference to a passage in Ezekiel before one group he was heard to confess that he could not believe what he could not understand, as he explained in his book on *Faith and Saving Faith.*

He could astound. On more than one occasion I watched him sit impassively as some student would attempt a question over and over again but never quite get it across because he had used some logical fallacy or other —totally confusing the great philosopher. Clark would merely point out the fallacy and sit in silence while the poor guy would try again. Often no other help would be offered at all, not even a word. He could appreciate people not having answers, but not being able to ask a question nearly always got him down . . . or was it just that he enjoyed making a point of rationality by his own silence?

Then there was the time when I moved him and his worldly possessions from Lookout Mountain where he had taught at Covenant College. He had insisted on riding with me in the truck all the way to Colorado, and he at age 82, by some reason of strength. It was one of the loveliest trips I ever took. His conversation was filled with stories and recollections. I had dreaded the prospect of my faulty questions going unanswered, or his school-teacher type corrections of my irrational utterances. On the contrary, he took interest in me, in the scenery, in people, billboards, weather, topography. By the time we had gotten to Illinois, my voice was worn out but he was as vigorous as when we started. It was in Kansas that he finally began to get quiet. In some desperation that Kansas would never end, I suggested that we use some time memorizing some portion of the Greek text, whereupon he reached for his briefcase, popped out his Nestle, and selected John 3:16 and following. Catechising each other for many miles, we went phrase by phrase until quite a bit was tucked in memory by both of us. Dr. Gordon H. Clark was a schoolboy again and completely happy. And to me, Kansas had never been so compressed.

Contrary to the impressions of some, Dad Clark had affections (we call them emotions). He wept when he did his part at our wedding; his voice wavered when he prayed at the ETS meeting at Westminster Seminary; his sermons had their moments of passion. His parting moments after visits to our home were highly controlled affairs and usually earlier than planned, I believe, in order to get a jump on his emotions and escape under philosophic control. Emotions were not trustworthy, were a cause of unpleasant outcomes, were to be relegated to the more negative of doctrines. Some of his emotions were connected to the intensity of love, some to disappointments in ecclesiology, some to ordinary frustrations, and some to sin. Whatever is the judgment in the future of Dr. Clark's theories of human makeup, I am sure that in the past he was keenly acquainted with grief and joy.

Clark so loved truly clever humor, and laughed heartily; he could also dish it out. Someone mentioned that a student at Sangre de Cristo Seminary in Colorado once asked him what advice he could give in seeking a wife. Clark replied that he should look for a woman who had lots of money and a good library! I saw his humor even as he criticized long hair and beards in the 60's, but then would speak against himself when he examined the Greek text of I Corinthians 11:16. On the one hand he would ardently express his opinion based upon social analysis, but on the other hand he was captive to the Word even if it argued against his opinions. His humor also manifested itself in his writings that not sparingly used the tools of irony and sarcasm, unexpected examples, similes, and stories.

I have heard several stories of his chess games, but mine is the only one I venture to tell. It was our first game soon after I began courting his daughter. I blew him away for about 45 minutes and was so proud; but then he recouped and won the game. It was later that I learned that my early moves were so erratic that he was totally baffled. But in 45 minutes he had programmed his brain to mine—for purposes of contest only. Never, ever, through the years of more chess games with me, did he fall in defeat. His victories in games, as challenges in vigorous debate, brought him much delight.

The Man I Remember

Sharon Ritchey Gingrich

As I have listened to people talk in tribute to Dr. Clark and read what has been written in memory of him, I do not see the man I knew. Yes, he was a tremendous scholar, and he will always be remembered as such. Yes, he held quite controversial philosophical views, and that distinctive will not quickly fade. But those are not the things I think he would want me to remember him by. Instead they are things that even people who never knew him could "remember."

I studied "History of Ancient Philosophy" with Dr. Clark during the second semester of my freshman year. Many people had told me that to attend Covenant and not study under Dr. Clark would be missing a once-in-a lifetime opportunity. They were right, but not merely for the sake of a missed educational experience.

Through that class I gained a deep respect for Dr. Clark. I was impressed with how detailed and well developed his philosophy was. I admired his dedication to and firm belief in his stand, as well as gaining an appreciation for his clear manner of writing on complex philosophies. (You guessed it; we studied from his text *Thales to Dewey*.)

That class, however, was more than a stimulus to my growing interest in philosophy; it was the beginning of a unique friendship.

Dr. Clark and I always talked after class. Our topics were as varied as they could be—why grass is frequently painted in purple, current student "dress codes," and the advantage of knowing French and German. You see, he knew both languages, but I knew only German. At first this was a disappointment to him but it quickly became his favorite thing to tease me about. Every book Dr. Clark gave me he autographed and then proceeded to pen something in French, his eyes sparkling to match his mischievous grin. Maybe someday I will learn enough French to understand what he really meant.

We had more than just the typical relationship of a professor and student limited to the campus classroom. In addition to our talks, I was able to visit him in Colorado during the summer. One Saturday my friend and I left the camp where we were working and headed to the Zellers, for a visit. Unknown to us he had quite a day planned. We stayed at the Seminary only long enough for a quick lunch and tour. Dr. Clark then directed us all around southern Colorado admiring with us some of the most beautiful places I have ever seen. At the end of a very full day, rather than allowing us to treat him to dinner, he took us out and then filled up our gas tank for the return trip. Much to his disappointment, we did not have another day for him to show us around his favorite state, Arizona.

A few months later I received a letter from Dr. Clark. He thanked me for the time we spent together and anticipated another such time the next summer if the Lord allowed. Well, neither one of us was able to tour Colorado that summer, but I do look forward with great anticipation to the next time we meet. Then we will truly enjoy the mountains of God's truth, and his grace that waters the driest desert.

The Cold Hard Facts

Ruth Bell Graham*

"Ruth," said an old high school friend who had been studying at a secular university, "you ought to lose your faith. It would do you good."

No one had ever suggested that to me before, and it took me completely by surprise. But the seed was planted and it began to bear fruit, slowly but relentlessly.

I cannot say that I became an atheist. It takes more faith to be an atheist than to believe in God. It was impossible for me to look at the heavens at night without realizing there had to be a Creator. But I could not be sure the Bible was God's message to man, and if I could not be sure of that, I could not be sure that Jesus was who He claimed to be.

I began to argue. I argued with anyone who was willing to argue. It got to where people would avoid me when confrontation was inevitable.

"Here comes Ruth," was the general opinion of my friends, "we're in for another argument."

They didn't understand: I wasn't arguing to win, I was arguing desperately to lose. I wanted them to come up with

*Reprinted by permission from *It's My Turn* by Ruth Bell Graham.

valid reasons that I was wrong and they were right.

At that time, I had been dating a senior reputed to be one of the most brilliant students on campus. It didn't take him long to realize my predicament.

"You're having problems with your faith, aren't you?" he asked one day.

"You can say that again!" I replied.

"Let's go and see so-and-so," he suggested, naming a deeply spiritual professor on campus.

I objected.

"He will talk with me, and pray with me, and it could even get a little emotional. I don't want that. All I want are cold, hard facts." I wanted to go see Dr. Gordon Clark, known for his logic, his unemotional brilliance. I felt he would give me nothing but the cold, hard facts.

Gordon Clark at the Vatican

Janet Glenn Gray*

I first met Dr. Clark at Trinity College in Palos Heights, Illinois in the early seventies at an Evangelical Theological Society meeting which I attended with my professor, Dr. Mary Crumpacker, a former student and special friend to Gordon and his family. That meeting was especially lively as Dr. Clark was featured in philosophical argument against Dooyeweerd's sphere-sovereignty which seemed to be favorably accepted at this C.R.C. school. Entire classes of philosophy were brought into the lecture hall to hear the address. Afterwards students and professors joined in a lively exchange of ideas.

The next meeting I remember well is another E.T.S. gathering at Trinity College and Seminary at Deerfield, Illinois. Dr. Clark gave a paper on aesthetics and the Christian which included a parody on Keats' *Ode on a Grecian Urn*. At the time Mary and I were in an adult Sunday School class on Space and Time. It was near the birthday of our teacher, which happens to be on April 1st, so we asked Dr. Clark if we could have a copy of the parody to give as a perfect birthday gift on space and time since that constitut-

*Author, *The French Huguenots: Anatomy of Courage*

ed the conclusion of the parody. He agreed, so Mary diverted Dr. Gil Cook and I placed the parody on the board the following week so we could all enjoy the joke.

At a plenary session following debate between Norman Geisler (a Thomist) and Erwin Lutzer (an absolute idealist), comments flew. After several speakers had agreed or disagreed with the delivered material, Dr. Clark was recognized, got to his feet with full dignity, and succinctly proclaimed to Dr. Geisler, "You have forgotten the Fall."

Another time Dr. Geisler, in a keynote address honoring Thomas Aquinas, said that if we didn't have a Protestant Pope, Clark and Henry (Carl F.H.) were at least Protestant Cardinals. Dr. Clark was honored at that particular E.T.S. meeting upon the eve of his retirement. The president-elect of the society introduced Dr. Clark with the following story, which I shall reconstruct as best I can from memory:

> It seems that the story got around that everyone knows Dr. Clark. With modesty Clark always vehemently denies this. One day a friend overheard a conversation in St. Peter's Square. Two men were pointing to the balcony above the Square where the Papal apartments are located. One man said to the other, "Who are those two men on the balcony?"
>
> The second man replied immediately, "I don't know who that man in the robe and funny round hat is, but that's Gordon H. Clark with him."

In the winter of 1972-73 we had Dr. Clark at our home in Valparaiso, Indiana for a series of talks on his forthcoming book on I Corinthians. We were pounding up the baseboards the night before so he could initiate the new family room which was dedicated to the Lord's work. It was a delight to have had such a fine beginning.

As I began working on a graduate research project on the French Huguenots, Mary Crumpacker and I decided to drive down to Indianapolis to check a few things with Dr. Clark. He welcomed us with warmth and was glad to help in any way he could. He helped with a particularly elusive idiomatic phrase in French and ended up by agreeing to edit the entire work the first time around. He made many essential suggestions, such as the need to strive for as many primary sources as possible. He provided an exciting foreword for the published edition.

Mrs. Clark always was very gracious to us as hostess and friend. She had the entire family over for dinner whenever we were in the area—especially on our trips through Lookout Mountain. The Clarks lived near the hang-gliding "jump-off," so we spent many hours watching the colorful sky gliders circle high above the valley, but within touching distance from us, it seemed. Not long before she died Mrs. Clark made a knitted soap turtle for our son and coin purses for our daughters.

Once after a weekend church meeting in Valparaiso we took Dr. Clark back home to "the Mountain," loaded in the van between three children and our dog Tinker. We told stories the entire sixteen hours it took us to haul a long trailer behind us. Clark always remembered to include the children in our games or conversations.

It has been quite a plus getting to know Dr. Clark's daughters, Lois and Betsy, and their families. We have spent many precious hours in work and discussion high above the Wet Valley in Colorado.

Over the past few years my husband Jim and I have taken two courses from Dr. Clark at Sangre de Cristo

Seminary where we learned a great deal about the Word of God, truth, the epistemological question, great church creeds, and the importance of Augustine. I have called Dr. Clark on numerous occasions to ask him questions on events, theological problems, and just general information. It's a pleasure to have had him as a friend with whom I could share ideas, manuscripts, and problems. We are grateful to have had a long, warm, personal friendship with a great scholar who remained a faithful man of God.

The Early Years

Anna Marie Hafer

Dr. Gordon Haddon Clark and I, as children, grew up in his father's church. As everyone knows, there are two types of ministers—the preacher type and the teacher type. Dr. David Scott Clark, Gordon's father, was the teacher type. He really knew his Bible and taught his parishioners well. Much of my knowledge of the Bible was learned from his preaching and from his teaching in Sunday School as I was privileged to be in his class for several years.

Dr. David Clark was a very human man and never was above doing the most humble things. Ours was a small church—Bethel Presbyterian Church at 19th and York Streets, Philadelphia. The members were not affluent, so the church had little money, but always paid its bills on time. At the request of Dr. Clark all other bills were paid before his salary was given him. He always was willing to work on a small salary to help the church's finances and all too often he used his own money to help those in his congregation who were in need.

But money was not his only way of helping others. One day he visited an ill member who was home alone. Probably she was feverish and wanted a glass of water. Dr.

39

Clark went to the kitchen and noticed a sink full of soiled dishes. He got the glass of water and gave it to the patient and left soon afterward.

A short time later a neighbor came in to see the ill woman and once more she asked for water. The neighbor went to the kitchen and there she noticed Dr. David S. Clark. He had not left the house, but had removed his coat, rolled up his sleeves, and was washing the soiled dishes left in the sink.

He always was appreciative of service given by his parishioners. Our church had a volunteer choir—no gowns, no extras. Occasionally Dr. Clark would go down to church on choir nights and after the practice was over he would invite all across the street to the drug store where he would treat them to sodas at his expense.

Our church could not afford a secretary or assistant minister, so Dr. Clark had much to do. He was a volunteer teacher at Tennant College—now part of the Philadelphia College of Bible, Langhorne, Pennsylvania. Since he received no remuneration for his time, the school allowed him to have one of their students a couple of afternoons a week and on Sundays when they taught Sunday School. This was part of the student's field service and was a great help to Dr. Clark with no cost to the church.

Dr. Gordon Clark's mother was the most gracious of women and loved by all. She was active in all church work, but her main interest was in teaching and helping young people come to the saving knowledge of Jesus Christ and in having them accept Him as their Saviour.

It was in this environment that Dr. Gordon Clark had the privilege of growing up. When Gordon was a little shaver, he conceived the idea of a lovely surprise for his parents. He got three potatoes and placed them on the shelf inside the furnace door where the coal was shovelled into the heater. When dinnertime came, Gordon went down to the cellar and brought up the three potatoes which he proudly presented to his parents as an addition to the meal.

But his pride was short-lived as his parents asked him where he got the potatoes and he admitted he took them from the corner grocery store. His parents reminded him that that was stealing. Next morning his mother took him by the hand and walked him down to the grocery store and he had to confess to the manager that he had stolen the potatoes. Remuneration was made and Gordon went home a sadder and less proud boy but, perhaps, one who had learned a very useful lesson.

Gordon enjoyed music, played an instrument, and could act up like a clown in plays, etc., but his chief interest was in books. He loved to write and to teach. As he taught philosophy, the subject could, at times, become boring to some students, so a few of the more precocious ones made signs. If they got bored, they would raise a sign saying "JOKE" so Dr. Clark would have to stop his lesson and tell some joke and thus lessen the tension of deep lessons. Then he could resume his teaching with renewed interest from his class.

Dr. Gordon Clark was just as much interested in teaching, studying, and writing as his father before him. One day he was involved in his work at home when his wife had to do an errand. Their first child, Lois, was a baby and was left in Gordon's care. He put her in the center of their big double bed and went about his work, completely forgetting her until he heard her cry as she fell out of bed—fortunately not hurt.

Gordon had a number of food likes and dislikes as most

of us have. When he and his family lived in Illinois, he still was sought after for speaking engagements in the Philadelphia area, so he and his wife frequently stayed at my home. One day he was quite ill—his throat was sore and he was to speak that evening. So he stayed in bed all day. His wife went visiting as there was nothing she could do for him and their time in Philadelphia was limited. I was employed, but so long as I had Philadelphia cinnamon buns and plenty of milk in the refrigerator, Gordon was happy. In late afternoon he got a throat treatment and was able to speak that evening.

Another of his food interests was Philadelphia scrapple. Today it probably is packaged and sent all over the U.S., but back in those days Gordon had to wait until he came to Philadelphia to get some of that cheap delicacy. Tomatoes were one of the things he most disliked, but he ate watermelon because of the color of it. Why the color of tomatoes would not help his dislike, one never knew.

He was a real scholar. Although he did not attend seminary, he studied Hebrew and Greek on his own and I understand passed the Hebrew tests with higher grades that those who had been in seminary classes. Although ordained as a minister in the Orthodox Presbyterian denomination, Gordon was not interested in being a pastor of a church, as he thought he could do more good reaching young people in college. In addition to that he made a practice of taking a young boy on an outing on Saturday afternoons and there on a one-to-one basis he was able to bring the claims of Jesus Christ to his young friends.

For a time he taught an adult Sunday school class in his father's church. I was privileged to be in his class. He used many illustrations, but one always remained in my mind. It was a poor illustration, a crude one, yet an effective one which I always remembered and which I used a number of times. It ran something like this. A certain church had a series of evangelistic services. At the end of a meeting when the invitation was given, a man came forward. He was counselled and readily accepted the Lord as his Saviour. The next evening the man returned for the service. At the end of the service the usual invitation was given and again this same man came forward. As he was being counselled he admitted having accepted the Lord the previous night but said he had sinned again that day.

The counsellor explained that the sin of one who has accepted the payment of Jesus Christ for his sins does not make the sinner lose his salvation. He loses fellowship with Jesus Christ until he repents, asks forgiveness and endeavors not to commit the same sin again.

The man went home happy. Next night he again came to the service and when the invitation was given that night, once again the same man came forward. The counsellor again tried to explain to the man the plan of salvation but in desperation said he wished he could cut off the man's head at the moment and be sure the man was saved. A very crude illustration, but it brought home to a number of people in the class that had been uncertain of their salvation and their fear of losing it just what was necessary for them to believe to have eternal assurance.

In Gordon's later years he decided to become a "Grandfather Moses" as he developed his artistic skills. He became quite a skillful artist, painting his beloved hills and mountains in Colorado. And so he passed his later years writing and painting.

A Wide and Deep Swath[*]

Carl F. H. Henry

Among articulate Christian philosophers on the American scene, none has addressed the broad sweep of contemporary concerns from an evangelical Protestant view more comprehensively than Gordon H. Clark. To introduce him, therefore, to philosophers unfamiliar with his work seems a somewhat belated effort, since most thinkers abreast of current options must somewhere have met and sampled Clark's writings. From his ready pen has come not only an incisive history of philosophy, but also pungent works on philosophy of science and philosophy of religion; a volume on historiography is now in preparation.

No aggressive and creative scholar is without his critics, and some of Clark's friends have at times charged him with being an absolute idealist, or a fatalistic determinist, or a speculative rationalist—for reasons we shall note. But he stands out above all else, in the contemporary philosophical milieu, as a champion of a personal God— God as a living, willing, speaking, acting Person—whose

*Reprinted from *The Philosophy of Gordon H. Clark,* 1968. The Trinity Foundation intends to reprint the entire book in the near future.

sovereign purposes are accomplished in human affairs, and Who has revealed Himself authoritatively in the Judeo-Christian Scriptures.

Clark is not primarily an apologist for the Christian faith, however; he is first and foremost a professional philosopher, examining the questions that secular thinkers have raised about the nature of ultimate reality, assessing the answers, and exhibiting the unsolved problems. If any feature dominates his contributions to learning it is a rigorous logic that continually seeks out and evaluates the reigning tenets of the age, and alongside their weaknesses exhibits the superiority of the Christian revelation. Sustained internal criticism of the non-Christian alternatives is the towering strength of Clark's writings, and gives them force and power beyond that of any apologists for the Christian religion who swiftly shift the argument to external considerations by a one-sided appeal to the biblical teaching.

Clark is presently working on a book on historiography*, motivated partly by the confused notions of history found in contemporary religious scholars like Barth, Bultmann, and Cullmann. Cullmann's book *Christ and Time*, he points out, offers no theory of time (as one finds in Immanuel Kant) but is really a discussion of history. Recent religious writers, Clark contends, compare very unfavorably with secular historiographers. His appraisal of both secular and religious approaches will not be completed before 1969.

Although Clark touches all branches of philosophy in his writings, the unifying idea is epistemology; he does not face the problems of philosophy from the standpoint of a

*Published in 1972 as *Historiography: Secular and Religious*

metaphysician. Some critics have therefore asserted that he is an absolute idealist. But he approaches no problem from a metaphysician's standpoint; on the controlling assumption that epistemology is basic, he insists that metaphysical questions cannot be answered without first straightening out epistemology. In this respect he is methodologically akin to Kant rather than to Bradley and Whitehead.

Clark's emphasis on a personal God as the Supreme Principle can doubtless be construed as Idealism; for him, reality is fundamentally and basically intellectual rather than physical. But he is far from an absolute idealist. In his recent book, *Karl Barth's Theological Method,* Clark commends Barth's attack on Hegelian idealism because its treatment of personality as a subsidiary concept that applies only to men results in the loss of divine personality.

Nor does Clark consider himself as a Personalist in the Lotze-Bowne tradition. Actually he shuns any speculative metaphysical designation of his position. What he has set about to say is that the God revealed and described in the Old and New Testaments decrees the events of history and has created man in His image. It follows that man must have *a priori* equipment—that learning, contrary to Aristotle and Locke, is not simply an empirical process. While Clark shares the emphasis of Plato and Kant that man's mind is not a blank, he is neither a Platonist nor a Kantian; with the Calvinistic theologians he insists on the fall and depravity of man. Conservative theologians insist that man is *born* with a sinful nature, not merely that he becomes sinful by imitating Adam; that is, man comes to life's experiences with an *a priori* moral tilt. If they are willing to admit that man is not born ethically a blank, asks Clark, why should they deny that man is not born intellectually a blank. Why not stress that man has *a priori* equipment, inborn categories of thought or innate ideas, that do not arise from experience, but without which he cannot think anything, and which control his reactions to experience? In brief, God is rational, says Clark, Jesus Christ is the Logos, the logic of God, and the laws of logic are part of the image of God.

Clark has always looked disdainfully at the pietistic notion that religion is a matter of the heart, not the head. His essay "On the Primacy of the Intellect" refuses to ground the case for theism in either volition or emotion, and the theme is developed in his article "Faith and Reason." Clark emphasizes that the significant element in religious truth is cognitive; that the distinction between heart and head is not at all biblical. Thinking is the highest human activity; modern philosophers like Bergson who say that life is deeper than logic are wrong.

The Christian doctrine of revelation was best expounded by the Protestant Reformers, Clark contends. "One does not find a good and complete theory of revelation until one comes to the Reformation. Calvin, Luther, and the other Reformers insisted on *sola Scriptura* and on the inerrancy of Scripture, as well as its being the sole source of our knowledge." The Thomistic view of natural theology has little value, as Clark sees it. "Even Thomas Aquinas admits that it yields no revelational material—any special revelation, any truth about salvation—and I do not think it even demonstrates the existence of God. While general revelation—that is a better term than natural theology—may provide the basis of man's responsibility, for specific directions as to how to think and how to act it is necessary to have verbal communication. Certainly there is no guarantee that anyone could deduce the correct implications from what is often called 'the mighty acts of God' unless God himself explained their significance. Only if there is a divine interpretation, only if revelation consists of words expressing intellectual content, do spectacular events become of practical significance. Verbal plenary inspiration provides the information one needs for everything."

Clark's interest in theological issues reaches back to childhood days. D.S. Clark, his father, was raised in a Reformed Presbyterian home, attended Princeton Theological Seminary when it was still a vigorous center of evangelical training, and then studied in Scotland for a year before a lifetime in the pastorate. For nearly fifty years he was pastor of Bethel Presbyterian Church in Philadelphia. For a dozen of these years he also lectured in theology at the Philadelphia Deaconess School. Gordon Haddon Clark—born August 31, 1902—recalls during his earlier years his father's preparation, page by page, of *A Syllabus of Systematic Theology,* which appeared in three successive editions. While there were few extended father-son conversations on theology, the elder Clark did teach his son the Westminster Shorter Catechism, and Clark "more or less" listened to his father's sermons in church. But he made himself fully at home among the 1500 books in his father's library. There he found Calvin's *Institutes of the Christian Religion,* John Laidlaw's *The Bible Doctrine of Man,* B.B. Warfield's books on major theological concerns, A.A. Hodge on the atonement, and many other scholarly works. During his father's illness, Clark preached in Bethel Church—he was then a senior at the university—and was elected an elder of the church, one of the youngest to be ordained there. In 1944 he was ordained a minister of the Orthodox Presbyterian Church and is now a minister in the Reformed Presbyterian Church, Evangelical Synod. In 1966 he was awarded an honorary doctorate of divinity by Reformed Episcopal Seminary, which had invited him to give the commencement address. Across the years Clark never lost his ties to young scholars entering the Christian ministry, and during the last four years on the University of Pennsylvania faculty, from 1932-36, he served also as lecturer in Reformed Episcopal Seminary in Philadelphia.

Clark's interest in philosophy first flowered on the campus of Pennsylvania. There he took his undergraduate studies, receiving his A.B., Phi Beta Kappa key, and medal of L'Alliance Française, in 1924. He was named instructor in philosophy, and studied in Heidelberg during the summer of 1927. He majored in Greek philosophy for the doctor's degree, conferred in 1929 a few months after his marriage to Ruth Schmidt. He served on the Pennsylvania faculty until 1936. From the first, his years on the Pennsylvania campus were fruitful and productive, and his knowledge of languages—Greek, Latin, German, and French—stood him in good stead. To professional journals he contributed a number of articles on Plato and Aristotle, and particularly on Plotinus. He studied at the Sorbonne during the spring semester of 1930. In 1931 with T.V. Smith of the University of Chicago he edited a sourcebook of *Readings in Ethics*, published by F.S. Crofts and Company; the volume went into numerous printings and a second edition. One of Clark's chapters on the ethical teaching of "Early Christianity" reflected his refusal, despite the prevalent modernist concessions of the time, to assimilate Christian ethics to Greek moralism.

Clark's decision in 1936 to accept the post of associate professor of philosophy at Wheaton College, Illinois, was hardly a surprise. He was fully aware that the modernist assault on Christian theism rested on speculative premises that could be countered effectively, and he was interested in preparing a generation of Christian scholars for serious intellectual engagement. Dr. J. Oliver Buswell, Jr., was Wheaton's president in those days, and not only took the academic duties of an evangelical campus seriously, but also cherished the hope of a Christian university.

During the years at Wheaton numerous publications appeared on which Clark had done exhaustive research and considerable writing while on the Pennsylvania campus. *Selections from Hellenistic Philosophy* was published in 1940, a volume of selections with valuable introductions to half a dozen of the Hellenistic schools. It won its place as a source book on early Greek philosophy, and the first edition was soon sold out; a paperback edition was reprinted as recently as 1966. To the book *Selections From Early Greek Philosophy*, by Milton C. Nahm, now at Bryn Mawr, Clark in 1934 contributed the chapter on Democritus and translated some material not previously in English. In 1941 he wrote chapters on Plato, Aristotle, and the Hellenistic age for the composite history of philosophy by Martin, Clark, Clarke and Ruddick, also published by Crofts; although now out of print, the textbook sold quite well for more than a decade, going through several printings.

As Clark's interest broadened from Greek philosophy to the history of philosophy, years passed in which he taught medieval and modern as well as ancient thought; he authored one of his finest successes, the volume *Thales To Dewey.* Published in 1957 by Houghton-Mifflin, it remains in wide demand. Should it go into a second edition, he would rework the Plato chapter to incorporate material from the Martin, Clark, Clarke and Ruddick composite now out of print.

The sovereignty of God is the cornerstone of Clark's theological outlook, and it was this doctrine of divine predestination that created tensions on the Wheaton campus. Clark's thesis is that expressed in an article on "Responsibility and Determinism." God wills *everything;* He decrees whatever comes to pass, and controls the actions of all His creatures. But He wills many things for other reasons than many finite creatures do.

Since Clark's interests even in the history of philosophy are mainly epistemological, he gave attention to the methods of the various sciences. This study resulted in 1952 in *A Christian View of Men and Things,* published by Eerdmans simultaneously with the Payton lectures, a condensation of the book, given at Fuller Theological Seminary. The volume's chapters on history, politics, religion, science, epistemology, and ethics summarize Clark's views of prevalent methods of approach and their results. Its exposition of ethics is the fullest we have from Clark's pen, and the dominant emphasis is that without a Christian theistic basis one not only fails to defend Christian ethics, but cannot erect any principles at all; life consequently becomes totally meaningless and useless.

While Clark has not altered the basic positions affirmed in *A Christian View Of Men and Things,* he has subsequently elaborated his view. The chapter on Science in *A Christian View* says hardly anything about operationalism, but in the paperback titled *The Philosophy of Science and Belief in God* he develops material only hinted at earlier, and takes a definite position on operationalism. On the subject of religion, which likewise occupies a chapter in *A Christian View,* Clark also has written a separate volume, *Religion, Reason, and Revelation* in which the outlines of the earlier chapter are considerably expanded. The material is more than an expansion, however; some earlier material, such as the appraisal of Edgar

Sheffield Brightman's view, drops out to avoid repetition.

Whether Clark is treating history or politics or ethics, or whatever else, the positive principle of his approach is supplied by the content of Scripture which provides the controlling ideas of his exposition. His forthcoming book on historiography aims to defend a biblical view of history. In *A Christian View of Men and Things,* the chapter on politics takes its principles from Scripture. Contrary to Sidgwick and many British moralists who defended what was to all outward appearances Christian ethics—in that it promoted certain Christian ideals without Christian theology at their base—Clark seeks to show, in his chapter on ethics, not simply that Christian ethics cannot be divorced from Christian metaphysics, but that no ethics of any kind can be defended on a non-Christian base. Neither the Utilitarians nor French existentialists like Jean Paul Sartre can defend their type of life on the basis they affirm. Sartre and the French existentialists generally turn out to be left-wing politicians with a dash of Communism—but their own principles, if consistently developed, would permit them no better defense of Communism than of Christianity or any other alternative.

Clark was born into a generation whose temper in secular philosophy was to undergo radical change. In the early part of the century, and even into Clark's student days, a great Hegelian tendency characterized many universities; some were totally Hegelian. What is now called Indiana State University at Terre Haute was founded explicitly on Hegelian principles. But after World War I Hegelianism was on the decline; today, very little of it survives. With the retirement at Yale a few years ago of Brand Blanshard, one of the last representatives of perhaps one of its best forms, Hegelianism has just about passed from the scene. The most coherent and vocal group in recent decades has been the logical positivists, perhaps more recently balanced by the logical and vigorous philosophers of analysis and the linguistic philosophers of Oxford. Apart from these movements nothing very distinguishable has arisen in contemporary philosophical thought.

The weakness of absolute idealism, as Clark sees it, was that the Hegelian categories never connected with actual science as practiced in the nineteenth century; toward the end of that century distinguished physicists like Vogt and Buchner reacted against Hegelianism and became outright materialists. The weakness of logical positivism is its empiricism. From an empirical theory, Clark stresses, one cannot derive a norm of any sort. To emphasize the uselessness of science outside its own limited sphere, Clark points out that "science cannot determine its own value . . . . By science bombs are made and cancer may soon be cured . . . . But can experimentation demonstrate that either the destruction of cities or the extension of life is good? The value of science depends on the value of life; but the value of life, and therefore the value of science itself, must be determined by some sort of general philosophy. And it is my conviction that . . . the only position that satisfactorily manages all these problems is the revelational philosophy of Christian theism."

Newtonian science, moreover, though it reared a magnificent structure, was based on certain self-contradictions which were swept away by Locke and Einstein. Clark finds linguistic philosophers differing so much among themselves that the vulnerable point varies from writer to writer, some of its proponents being utterly pedantic. While some linguistic material has value, he concedes, one cannot move from it to epistemological or metaphysical content. Moreover, certain recent theories of religious language are simply false; they are based, Clark notes, on an empirical and evolutionary view of the origin and development of language, and the underlying principles cannot actually be carried through to a coherent system of thought. In *Religion, Reason and Revelation* (1961) Clark defended a theistic view of language as a gift of God that begins with spiritual categories, instead of projecting concepts of the supernatural by analogy out of materialistic factors.

Clark does not see any signs of a return to Christianity on a wide basis in the intellectual arena. But his analysis of secular philosophy has never been answered by the professional philosophers, despite Clark's repeated assault on their positions. Clark shows that secular philosophy leaves life without meaning and in utter frustration. But if the revealed God is taken as the first principle, a theory of epistemology and of history gains positive content, and life gains significance—including personal destiny for eternity. Revelation, in brief, creates the possibility—and the only possibility—of living a life that one can regard as significant, as meaningful, as worth living. Few contemporary philosophers and theologians have chosen to take cognizance of Clark's work, but for a full generation he has exposed the deficiencies of their alternatives to Christian faith. Those who have tangled with him in public debate know how skillfully he turns the discussion to epistemological issues, and shows that rival theories rest not on an intellectual demand but on emotive, volitional or speculative considerations. In an age when human history is at a critical crossroads the case for Christian theism, as Clark vindicates it, deserves larger hearing and fuller reply than it has enjoyed. For, while they may differ with Clark's position in certain details, many evangelical Protestant scholars are convinced that the silence of professional philosophers is an unwitting tribute to the validity of his views. The silence may, of course, also indicate a lack of interest in the case for Christian theism. But it is to be expected of man as sinner— and also supplies confirmation of the scriptural revelation of man and life. In any event, Gordon H. Clark is not only one of the profoundest evangelical Protestant philosophers of our time, but he has also blessed the Church of Christ and particularly young scholars seeking to relate Christianity and contemporary thought with a rich legacy of disciplined thought and writing. It has been my privilege to study under him, to have read almost all of his writings, and to have known him as a friend. I count it a distinct honor to contribute this introduction to the Clark *Festschrift*. In the confused intellectual jungle of our age, Clark has cut a deep swath for the Christian revelation. Those who have not yet read his works have a rewarding opportunity awaiting them.

A Colleague and Player of Chess

J.C. Keister*

When I was asked to write of my experiences with
Gordon Clark, I eagerly accepted. My wife and I sat down,
reminisced, and constructed a list of incidents which had
occurred over the years we had known him. These incidents can be categorized, of course, and I found myself
outlining our memories of Gordon along the following
lines:

1. Gordon's generosity
   a. incident #1
   b. incident #2
2. Gordon's humor
   a. incident #1
   b. incident #2
   etc.

When I was through, I had completed the equivalent
of a series of axiomatic "proofs" of Clark's generosity,
humor, etc., all of which could be presented in an appropri-
ate mathematical form by chapter, section and sub-para-
graphs. I am not certain that Gordon would necessarily
disapprove of the organization (although he might be

*Former Professor of Physics, Covenant College, Lookout Mountain,
Georgia.

embarrassed that we had written about such things at all), but it is not at all clear that a reading audience would appreciate a biography written along the lines of a textbook in Euclidean Geometry.

What should be done? Some snapshots? Descriptions of past incidents? After all, as Gordon himself stated when writing about historiography, the best one can hope for in summarizing the history of a nation or individual is to reach into a grab bag of past events and write about them as best you can. So, we will do just that and for a man as complex as Gordon Clark, perhaps that is the best way to pay him tribute.

Gordon's Opinions on This and That
1. Athletic events are the lowest form of human activity. They are, however, fun to watch.
2. Electric stoves are barbaric. Only gas stoves are civilized.
3. The gymnasium should be turned into a large spectator arena for chess, after which Bobby Fischer should be invited to attend.
4. The guitar is an inferior musical instrument.
5. Only unpolished flour is suitable for making French bread.
6. Chess is the highest form of civilized activity.
7. Scientific theories are a collection of useful falsehoods.
8. Music is the lowest form of artistic communication, and literature is the highest form.
9. While in college, a student's sanctification and his standing before God depend on his getting and maintaining a 4.0 average.
10. Girls who wear jeans are uncivilized.
11. Cheerleaders should be allowed at basketball games only if chess is played at half time.

Gordon's Generosity and Good Nature

Besides the encouragement he gave me in my studies, Gordon also was generous with his possessions. For example, when he was teaching in Colorado for several months, he loaned us his car. He gave us a chest freezer one time. During the last few years of his life (before he moved to Colorado), he sold his house and moved into an apartment. He invited me over to give me my choice of paintings, garden tools and other belongings he had. He had a similar reputation on Lookout Mountain among the residents there, who all thought very highly of him.

"Red" Powell—a mechanic who lived 2½ miles south of Covenant College—would frequently ask the college students about "that very nice old man, who would talk and joke around." "Shorty" Moore—another Lookout Mountain businessman—always identified Gordon as a "very nice man."

Chess and All That

It was a Monday night after supper when the phone rang. Susie answered, and indicated that I would be able to return the call in a few minutes. She then turned to me, with her inimitable giggle, and relayed the phone message: A little boy wants to know—"Can J.C. play chess tonight?" Well, Gordon Clark was the only "little boy" I knew who would make a request like that, so I sat down and phoned him back to start our nightly telephone chess game.

I had (by that time) lost count of the number of games we had played, but it had to have been in the dozens. And I mean games played over the phone. This may explain a lot to some of our former students who tried to contact us at home by phone and found the line busy from 8:00 P.M. on. (After all, one can't interrupt a chess game at move 35 to discuss math or philosophy, can one? Priorities are priorities!) I remember one game lasting from 8 to 12—a draw, as it turned out.

For those of you who like chess and who live some distance from your favorite chess partner, I highly recommend telephone chess. What with "paging" systems that the phone companies have these days, I don't think you'll miss many calls. And if you have someone as good as Gordon to play, how can you lose?

Gordon's Artistic Bent

Gordon, as most of us know, spent a good deal of time painting. My wife asked him about this once: "Do you like painting?" And his response was: "Oh, I work at it!" I am very honored to have some of his paintings. Now, his talents in philosophy far exceeded his talent in painting, but his paintings were still quite good.

He had artistic bents in other directions, too. One of the most interesting was demonstrated during a Chapel talk at Covenant College. Gordon was called upon to introduce Carl F.H. Henry. Gordon (as well as Dr. Henry) was on the stage at the time, and he walked over to a table on which rested two medium sized boxes. He opened one box, and proceeded (without saying a word) to withdraw books, one at a time, and stack them on the table. When he had finished the first box, he pitched it to the floor and opened the second box, continuing the book-stacking process. It slowly dawned on the audience that these books had all been written by Dr. Henry, and that this was Gordon's way of showing the extent of Dr. Henry's scholarship. At the end of the book stacking operation (when several dozen books had been piled up, one on top of the other, in two separate stacks), Gordon simply stated:

"I would like to introduce Dr. Carl F.H. Henry, one of the most prolific and distinguished scholars in the evangelical community." I don't think one can beat that for a graphic and artistic introduction of a speaker!

The Girl In the Classroom
Many of Gordon's classes had a preponderance of men in them, which distressed Gordon. After all, he (like most men) liked the charm of the company of women. However, as indicated in the Clark opinion section, women needed to be dressed in a proper way.

One day, at the beginning of one of his introduction to philosophy classes, one of his female students (a rather attractive young lady) arrived with a fancy blouse and blue jeans. Gordon, naturally, had strong conflicting feelings about all this, and remarked, "You look very good from the waist up!" This completely broke up the class. The girl went up to Gordon and kissed him on the cheek, whereupon he beamed.

John Gildernew, (who had a full beard at the time), exclaimed, "If I had said something like that, I would have got my face slapped!"

Gordon promptly replied, "Well, Gildernew, if you shaved, you might get a girl to kiss you!"

Two and one-half years later, at a Sunday dinner at the College president's house, Gildernew announced his engagement to the president's daughter. Gordon leaned over to him and said, "I see you found a girl who would kiss you!"

Memory and good humor, both!

Advice on the Mathematics Article
I had known Gordon for two to three years when I sat

down with John Sanderson at a table in the Krystal store in Chattanooga. John was leaving Covenant College to take a position at Covenant Seminary, and I wanted to glean as much as I could from him before he left. Covenant College emphasizes the principle that the Bible is the basis of all knowledge, (including math and physics, which I taught). At the time, I was skeptical. Wasn't there some "neutral" ground? Some areas of knowledge where one's belief system was unimportant? It seemed to me at the time that it really didn't matter what you believed as long as you did your calculations correctly. Mathematical axioms were true and the Bible didn't really have much to say about them.

At least that's what I thought then. When I expressed my concerns to John, he promptly gave me some counter examples in other areas (*e.g.,* a speech instructor who laid the foundations for evolution at the start of a speech class). Sure, sure; but what about math? John didn't know specifically what to do to determine how math could be developed Biblically, but he insisted that it could be done. He also stated that we all were at best babies in our understanding of how to go about constructing a biblical basis for most areas of endeavor, and that we needed to get moving.

"So how do I get started in math?" I demanded.

"Well, talk to Gordon Clark," John said. "Even he is a toddler, in terms of what ultimately can be done, but he is at least walking. He won't be with us too many more years, so you be sure you pump him for everything you can get."

So I went to Gordon to chat about the problem. He said "Yes, it can be done."

"How?" I asked.

"You need to read the Bible using standard exegetical methods to do it," he said. "And keep mathematics in mind when you do it," he added.

Big help! I thought.

Well, I was reading Matthew at the time, and I opened up to Matthew 17. Toward the end of the chapter, there was a section dealing with Peter's encounter with the temple officials; you know the temple tax question. If you recall, Peter was asked, "Does your master pay the two drachma tax?" and Christ's response included, "in his [the fish's] mouth you will find a [four drachma] piece—use it to pay for your tax and mine." Well, now! Doesn't this state that 2 X 2 = 4? I went back to Gordon about it and he smiled: "Keep it up! Keep it up!" So I started at the beginning with Genesis: "Adam lived 130 years and had Seth . . . and he lived 800 years after that. He lived 930 years and he died." Hmmmm. . . . 130 + 800 = 930. . . .

And it went on from there.

What about the arithmetic axioms? It turns out they are in Scripture, too, although some of them need to be established by standard exegetical methods, just as one would do for many other doctrinal principles from Scripture. (Yes, many mathematical principles can be derived as doctrine from Scripture just like other thoughts involving our lives!) Gordon was encouraging me all the way and then I received a letter from John Robbins. Unbeknownst to me, Gordon had cleared the way with John Robbins for me to write an essay about the Biblical foundations for mathematics. Both Gordon and John encouraged, criticized, and otherwise helped shepherd the essay through publication.

Many thanks were due to both men, but to Gordon especially for "seeing me through" from the start. I shan't forget Gordon!

Gordon Clark, a Teacher

Deborah Pattison Kozlowski

My connection with Dr. Clark begins before I was born. My father seriously studied philosophy as a hobby and says he was especially "enamored of Kierkegaard" in his early years. However, by the grace of God, he became a Christian after reading some of Dr. Clark's books. So, in a sense, Dr. Clark is responsible for my Christian upbringing which led to my salvation. (He baptized my sister and me at the Indianapolis Reformed Presbyterian Church in the early 1960s.)

I arrived at Covenant College in 1978. Dad had informed me that I had to take philosophy courses from Dr. Clark. It was an opportunity, he said, to study at the feet of a master. Since he was paying the tuition, I couldn't argue. Besides, he had insisted on Latin in high school and I had enjoyed that in spite of initial misgivings.

I first renewed acquaintance with Dr. Clark on campus and at the Lookout Mountain Reformed Presbyterian Church. He was always very cordial and assured me there was nothing to fear about college philosophy courses. In addition, he had a reputation for being kinder to girl students.

Modern Philosophy was the first course I took. I found

most of the issues baffling at first. My brain hurt after the hour-and-a-half sessions each Tuesday and Thursday. He lectured from his book, *Thales to Dewey,* and asked numerous questions of his students. Most of us were too confused to give meaningful answers, but we did learn quickly not to fake a reply. He had absolutely no patience with jargon or catch phrases (which a number of the Bible majors could use easily). He would press hard to find exactly what the student meant by a phrase and insist that the proper meaning of words be used at all times. This emphasis on precise language would be one of his main contributions to his students. We did appreciate and recognize it, even though his relentlessness could be embarrassing and frustrating. He had us work hard to understand the basic arguments, but that was never enough. He pushed us to use and apply them. Each philosopher was a new challenge.

He sponsored a Bible study on I John at his home at the beginning of the course. (Unfortunately, it died after a few weeks since only about two students in twenty had cars.) After the initial session, I complained to my diary that he constantly tried to tug knowledge out of us—even if it wasn't there. He was charming and informative, in spite of the intellectual rigor he imposed, and encouraged questions. We dorm students also appreciated his generosity in opening his home and in scooping out enormous dips of ice cream.

His quizzes (he refused to call them tests, even though students complained that quizzes implied trivial exams) weren't as terrifying as I had expected. He would write three to six questions on the board and we were to write as much as we could in reply. Detailed study of the text always insured excellent grades. He assigned points to each of the questions based on the thoroughness of the answer (and, we decided, the number of pages covered). I did well, after all, and teased him about giving me extra points because of our friendship. He informed me that he was too fair to bestow special favors.

The one exception to the "more is better" rule was in an essay on the final objection to empiricism. I wrote a page and a half; he scrawled across the page that this much information was a waste of space.

His pre-class prayers were careful, expressive, and tremendously reverent. He graded in either fountain pen or red crayon. His handwriting was almost indecipherable.

As we studied Descartes, Spinoza, Locke, Hume, theories of existence, causality, perception, and necessity, it became obvious that he had little use for empiricism, but he really didn't discuss his own philosophical system much at all. We were too ignorant to ask very searching questions in the beginning, but over the semester (and in the Bible Study) we learned of the law of contradiction, what the Johannine Logos really means, the uselessness of sensations, and the necessity (for a Christian and a philosopher) to accept the Bible as our presupposition.

By the time I took Ancient Philosophy, a year and a half later, I was a bit more knowledgeable of the general issues and more comfortable with his style to settle down and do some serious learning.

His class lectures were always stimulating, whether or not he kept to the subject at hand. In addition to his searching analyses of Kant and Anaxagoras and Parmenides, his familiarity with an incredible range of subjects always interested and impressed us. We learned to ask his opinion on books to be read, the effectiveness of a particular argument, the quality of bear steaks in Colorado, and the techniques of drawing circles. Here are some quotes from my notes:

The process of a college education is learning less and less until you know absolutely nothing.

It's very bad to be imaginative.

Descartes made a mess of getting existence.

You're not educated until you've taken courses in German.

I like ladies singly or in groups.

Philosophy doesn't deal with unfamiliar things; it deals with familiar things, and that is why it puzzles you.

Psychology is not a science; it's a mess.

Berkeley annihilates one part of Locke and Hume annihilates the other.

Pain is not a quality of a hammer (after you've been hit on the head). Why is red a quality of tomato?

Carl Henry is improving on his Greek philosophy.

Why didn't the Romans stay in Tyre and Phoenicia? Why did they have to come to Italy and mess things up for 2000 years? (Clark was speaking of substance.)

Theology is a bit more complicated than chess; one should have to defeat Bobby Fischer before being deemed a competent theologian.

Dr. Clark's rigorous and uncompromising beliefs did spark animosity as well as admiration among some students and professors on campus. My Apologetics professor had Dr. Clark explain his philosophy to our class one session. After Dr. Clark completed his lecture, responded to questions, and left, the professor said his method of apologetics was heresy and no one would likely come to salvation after hearing the Gospel preached by Dr. Clark. I argued with the professor concerning his analysis of Dr. Clark and cited my father as an example to the contrary.

It was in the course on Apologetics that I got to study Dr. Clark's system of philosophy in greater depth. We had to write a paper on any system of apologetics. Dad said, "Of course you should write on Dr. Clark; your source is right there." So I began reading his books and interviewed him several times in the college cafeteria (he ate there to get his salad which he disliked but said he needed at his age). I asked my fumbling questions, he answered (much nicer than in class), told me questions that I should be asking, and answered them too. He edited my final draft and corrected words incorrectly or sloppily used. It was all terribly helpful and enlightening. He even complimented me on the paper (which meant more since he never used words carelessly!). His only suggestion was that I should have organized it into subtopics instead of writing one long narrative. Unfortunately, I didn't follow that since the fourteen-page paper was already typed, but I have followed that advice in subsequent papers on other subjects.

By my senior year we had a cordial and friendly relationship. I had no more room in my schedule to take philosophy courses and complete the requirements of my biology major, but I saw him on Sundays, around campus, and in the cafeteria. He was thinner and visited the doctor more often.

My family usually ate a meal with Dr. Clark on their annual trip to Lookout Mountain to deliver the next Pattison student. My youngest brothers, eight and ten at the time, thought Dr. Clark was a real comedian for asking the waitress for flashlights to see the food in a dimly lit restaurant. He flirted with my mother, asking her to go out west with him. My Korean roommate was impressed with his friendliness when he greeted her by bowing deeply, but she corrected him, explaining that while Japanese bow deeply, Koreans only bow slightly.

Dr. Clark never hesitated to give advice. My boyfriend came to visit me from Baltimore on a fairly regular basis. Dr. Clark wanted to know what his intentions were (marriage) and what mine were (I wanted more time). He told me that older men were better since girls matured faster than boys (Dennis is 5 years older) and that he didn't believe in long engagements. Dennis immediately decided he liked Dr. Clark. (We did get married and compromised on a wedding halfway through my senior year.)

Dr. Clark's classes have had a lasting effect in a number of ways. I constantly remember his insistence on precise language, whether it be listening to a minister (Christians can be very sloppy) or writing a memo at work or in conversation. His books have contributed to Sunday School lessons written by both my husband and me. Dennis has used him as a source for papers required in seminary courses. I know what a presupposition is and will remember the importance of the law of contradiction.

A Theological Giant

Harold Lindsell

I met Gordon Haddon Clark for the first time when I was a student at Wheaton College. He had taken a doctor of philosophy degree from the University of Pennsylvania, and when he came to Wheaton to teach he was in his early thirties. He was a Presbyterian who was steeped in the theology of John Calvin and could be said to be a firm adherent of what is familiarly called the TULIP doctrine.

From the first time I met Dr. Clark I knew that he was a thoroughgoing predestinationist who started with the doctrine of election and who followed it rigorously to its ultimate conclusion. He was, therefore, a believer in a particular or limited atonement, i.e., that Christ died only for the elect. He was equally certain that those elected would persevere. Holding these views, he was willing and able to take on all who disagreed with him. In his discussions he demonstrated a knowledge of the Word of God that was not only extensive but which was based on a knowledge of Greek and the ability to exegete it carefully. He was familiar with the nuances of the Word of God so that even the smallest jot or tittle could be advanced to support the claims he made.

No one on the Wheaton campus excelled Dr. Clark in

71

the field of logic. In all of his excursions into the field of theology logic was the focal point of reference. And he used it devastatingly. He was a master of the law of contradiction and insisted that if something was A it could not be not-A. He never for one moment believed that it was possible to accept paradox as a legitimate part of knowledge or of reason. He fought tenaciously against those who were willing to believe that opposites could both be true simultaneously. Whoever functioned this way was thought by him to entertain self-contradictory conclusions, and this he could never assent to.

While Dr. Clark was teaching at Wheaton he gathered around him a coterie of students who enthusiastically adhered to the viewpoint he supported. For the most part they also were open advocates of views they were willing to talk about and argue for and if need be die for. He and they were controversialists in the best sense of that term and were convinced that the matter at stake was of supreme importance for a Christian.

For Dr. Clark and those who rallied around him the chief enemies of the position they held were the Arminians who negated all five points of TULIP. The Arminians did not start with election, nor did they believe in irresistible grace, a particular or limited atonement, or total depravity. Moreover they believed that one who had been saved could lose his or her salvation, *i.e.*, they did not believe that once saved was to be always saved. My own personal questions revolved around the accuracy of two opposing viewpoints. This introduced another factor in my own personal life about which something should now be said.

I was a history major at the college and the curriculum did not include any required courses in philosophy, which was the area of Dr. Clark's competence. I was not a pre-seminary student and at that time had no sense of a divine call to the ministry. My relationships with Dr. Clark revolved around chess. He and Mrs. Clark maintained an open house for students, and hordes of them enjoyed the privilege of sitting in their living room conversing with them and with the students who roomed in the Clark residence. At that time most of the students lived off campus in private homes and many of the professors rented out rooms to students. This was true of the Clarks. It so happened that Dr. Clark was a skillful chess player who met and conquered lesser mortals whose knowledge and abilities in this field were not to be compared with his. I played many a game of chess with Dr. Clark and was beaten again and again by him. On one occasion he was playing four or five games of chess at the same time. I was quickly defeated and engaged myself in a conversation with Mrs. Clark in the kitchen. Her husband could hear what we were saying and I had her in a theological corner, which was obvious to Dr. Clark. He got so upset that he lost one of the games of chess and rushed out to the kitchen and summarily told his wife to leave me to him. Then ensued a somewhat heated debate which put me at a severe disadvantage with one whose gifts and knowledge were far beyond those of a mere college student. This conversation was related to another aspect of my life during my college days.

I have mentioned Arminianism and thereby hangs the tale. I was friendly with another professor in the English department. I never took a course under him any more than I had under Dr. Clark. Yet these two men had as much influence on my thinking, present and future, as any two people on campus. That Arminian was Dr. Lauren King who had a Ph.D. degree from Ohio State University and was a man of many gifts. He was just as resolutely an Arminian as Dr. Clark was a Calvinist. And never the twain did meet. Again and again I would go from the one to the other torn with doubts as to which viewpoint I could make peace with, and which of two masterful men had the better of the argument. This was a time of theological education for me and brought me face to face with something I knew to be true—the Arminian and the Calvinist positions were antithetical and could not be reconciled. These sturdy supporters of two basically opposed theological systems made it necessary for me to grapple with the history which lay beneath two different systems of thought. I learned that Calvinism was challenged in, of all places, Holland, by one who had been raised in the Reformed tradition and dissented from it.

Jacobus Arminius (Jakob Hermandszoon) was a renowned and able Dutch Reformed theologian who lived from 1560 to 1609. His father was a cutler. Jacobus the son studied at Utretch and for a time at Marburg. When he heard that most of his relatives had been slaughtered by the Spaniards he returned to Holland and took refuge at Rotterdam. This was followed by studies at Leyden, Geneva, Basel, Padua, and Rome. In 1587 he was back in Holland, was ordained a year later, and served a church in Amsterdam. His study in the book of Romans brought doubts to his mind about the doctrine of predestination. Little did he know that his departure from Calvinism would lead after his death to the Synod of Dort in 1618-1619 and the teaching of "double" predestination of some to life and others to death. As his views began to change, Arminius was charged with Pelagianism and a departure from the confessions of his church. When the struggle to unseat him did not succeed, it was followed by a more pronounced opposition to Calvinistic doctrines. In 1603 he was appointed a professor at Leyden and was engaged in serious theological controversy until his death.

Arminius persisted in his opposition to Calvinism by his efforts to secure a revision of the Belgic Confession and the Heidelberg Catechism. He did not succeed in this endeavor but he was successful in turning a number of his fellow-believers away from supralapsarian or sublapsarian views of predestination which he regarded as unbiblical. Hugo Grotius, the famed expert in international law, was one of his students and an ardent advocate of the views entertained by his professor. The year after Arminius's death in 1609 *The Remonstrance* was published. It was drawn up at Gouda in the presence of 46 ministers. Its authorship has been disputed but some thought it was written by Grotius. The Arminian document was condemned by the Synod of Dort in 1618-1619.

It can be said that Arminianism, which wholly opposed the TULIP of traditional Calvinism, did not die. Its influence through those who adopted it in whole or in part can be seen in the Dutch and European Protestant theological movements of this modern age. It was certainly strongly felt in England where John Wesley was one of its most notable adherents. English and American Methodism was and still is Arminian in its theological system. Clark, in his life and ministry, was faced with the formidable task of defending Calvinism against a rising tide of Arminianism.

Clark was aware of the fact that evangelical Christianity in America in our generation could not be said to be either genuinely Calvinistic or Arminian. Most of those who professed to stand in the Reformed tradition were logically inconsistent. When they held to an unlimited atonement and free will they, of necessity, were emptying predestination and election of any real meaning by Clark-ean standards. And by the standards of logic, it may be said. It can be likened to the impasse occasioned by the teachings of Augustine and Pelagius, the first of whom can be said to have been a Calvinist and the other an Arminian. The result of that struggle led to Semi-Pelagianism, not unlike the conflict we face today. Most evangelicals are not consistent Arminians or Calvinists. They are generally either Semi-Arminians or Semi-Calvinists. This can easily be demonstrated.

Clark Pinnock illustrates the uneven journey between the poles of Calvinism and Arminianism. Somewhat like Harvey Cox of Harvard, of whom it can be said that he has a new theology every day, Pinnock has wrestled himself into a clearly paradoxical position which has brought him into strong opposition to Gordon Haddon Clark's Calvinism. At one time Pinnock was more or less in the Refo-med tradition. He has now moved farther and farther away from that position into the Arminian camp. In connection with this movement away from the Reformed tradition he ran right into a theological dilemma regarding the omniscience of God and the free will of man. This is what he said:

> . . . Cottrell insists on holding to God's timelessness and total omniscience. Apparently God from his timeless vantage point can see the whole reel of time all at once, including the contingent acts yet to be done. To me this is not compatible with the Arminian belief in genuine human freedom. If God knows infallibly what I will do tomorrow, then I do not have the freedom to do otherwise. It will not do to say God did not determine it but only foresaw it. The action is as fixed and necessary as if God decreed it. Cottrell has walked into the arms of the Augustinians who know that total omniscience and timelessness imply determin-

ism. I see no way around "limiting" omniscience to what CAN be known (*i.e.,* not future contingents). (*TSF Bulletin,* September-October 1984, p. 31.)

Dr. Pinnock is quite clear what the choices are: either "genuine human freedom" or the "limited omniscience" of God. By suggesting "limited omniscience" he is engaged in a contradiction. He has reduced God to something more manlike. We too know some things for sure and do not know other things. Such being the case, we simply are not omniscient. Dr. Pinnock has emptied the word *omniscient* of its real meaning as any dictionary will show to be true. For example, *Webster's Ninth New Collegiate Dictionary* says that the word means "having infinite awareness, understanding and insight" or "possessed of universal or complete knowledge." If God is not omniscient, he is not really God. Moreover Pinnock of necessity would have to say that Christ's date on the cross of Calvary could not have been known in advance by the Father. It was a future contingent and thus beyond even the ken of God. But this denies what the Scripture teaches about Christ as the Lamb of God slain before the foundation of the world (Revelation 13:8).

What does this have to do with Gordon Haddon Clark? A great deal. Professor Pinnock is not only fighting against Augustine, who was indeed, like John Calvin, a predestinarian. He is also fighting against Clark who has stood in the tradition of Augustine and Calvin for many years. The Trinity Foundation published a book by Clark titled *Clark Speaks From the Grave.* It was reviewed by Clark Pinnock in the *TSF Bulletin,* May-June 1987 (p. 37). This is what Dr. Pinnock wrote:

This is a bizarre book, and I do not recommend it. The

author is not in fact Gordon H. Clark but rather his devoted disciple John Robbins who speaks for the late author against his critics in this nasty little diatribe, called a "post-humous" lecture. Underlying the book (really a booklet) is an incredible admiration for Clark as one of the great, if not the greatest, Christian philosopher-theologian of all time. Supremely confident and pretentious, this "voice" from beyond cuts down all the wicked critics of Clark's ideas, most denizens with him of the sectarian Presbyterian sub-culture in America. Obviously we have not heard the last of Gordon Clark, since a foundation has been established to publish and republish his work. I am a little disappointed, because I had hoped that with his death this Clark would have rested in peace, and we too would have some relief from his weird combination of pure rationalism [sic] dark predestinarian ruminations. No such luck!

Never mind the ineptness of the professor's grammar and faulty use of words. Let's look at the contents of his statement. First and foremost he could hardly have failed to note that indeed the material in the book was written by Dr. Clark himself. But he did! And John Robbins wrote nary a word of the material itself. Dr. Pinnock calls this work a "nasty little diatribe," something defined in the dictionary as "a bitter and abusive speech or writing." Dr. Clark was neither bitter nor abusive in his writing or in his conduct. He was straightforward and tough to be sure. He called a spade a spade. He had no use for viewpoints that called Calvinism into question, but nowhere did he suggest that those who disagreed with him had no right to their viewpoints. Had Professor Pinnock preceded him in death one can be sure that Gordon Haddon Clark would never have used the words about him that he used about Dr. Clark.

Dr. Clark's logic was no less logical than that employed by Dr. Pinnock. Their differences lie in their presuppositions, not their logic. Dr. Clark believed in the omniscience of God and therefore concluded that the free will of Dr. Pinnock is not sustainable with a belief in omniscience. Dr. Pinnock started from the presupposition that man has free will or the power of contrary choice and this presupposition led him logically to conclude that God cannot know everything before it is done by men. In this sort of situation Clark looks better than Pinnock, who has used violent and unrestrained language against a fellow-Christian. There are many full-blooded Arminians who are in total disagreement with Dr. Clark, but few, if any, of them would speak about this theological giant in the language employed by Dr. Pinnock.

It is important for those who are uncommitted to either position to understand more completely what it means to hold the position articulated by Dr. Pinnock. Then they will be better able to contrast that position with the one held by Dr. Clark. A short list of what God could not have known will help:

1. God could not have known in advance whether Mary would or would not have agreed to be a participant in the incarnation of the Son of God.

2. God could not have known whether Joseph would respond to the will of God to become the protector of the innocent virgin and thus offer her protection from the scandal of being an adulteress.

3. God cannot know in advance whether anyone will respond to the gospel invitation and accept Jesus Christ as Savior and be born again. Indeed no one may respond and all may be lost.

4. God could not have known what He says He did

know in the case of Jeremiah. "Now the word of the Lord came to me saying, 'Before I formed thee in the womb I knew you, and before you were born I consecrated you; I appointed you a prophet to the nations' " (Jeremiah 1:4-5).

5. God could not have known in advance whether Saul would respond to the gospel invitation in Acts 9.

These are only a few examples of what God could not have known. The list can be enlarged hundreds of times from the Old and New Testaments. When the implications of Dr. Pinnock's position are unfolded any Christian is then free to choose between Pinnock or Clark. There are many Arminians who accept the full omniscience of God and the free will of man without worrying about the apparent inconsistency. Dr. Pinnock is not one of them. He uses the same kind of logic employed by Gordon Clark to repudiate God's full omniscience and retain man's free will. Dr. Clark, however, accepts God's complete omniscience and lets go of man's free will as understood by Dr. Pinnock. Dr. Pinnock declares that his viewpoint gives him "some relief from [Dr. Clark's] weird combination of pure rationalism [sic] dark predestinarian ruminations." If it is rationalistic to vote for Clark against Pinnock in these circumstances, so be it!

It is fair to say there are two Gordon Haddon Clarks. One is the giant who entered the fray in defense of Calvinism against men like Pelagius and Arminius. This was Clark the theologian speaking from Scripture and dealing with revelation. As a theologian he always placed revelation over human reason. He used human reason to be sure, but it was controlled by revelation. He submitted his human reason to the Word of the living God. His mind and his reason were captive to Scripture. Always and ever his final or bottom line was "What does the Bible say?" Once he accepted the Bible as the unerring Word of God he used his reason to challenge any and all who said the Word of God is erroneous in any of its parts. In one instance in doing this he paid Clark Pinnock of whom we have just spoken a fine compliment. This occurred in chapter 8 of his book *God's Hammer: The Bible and Its Critics.*

In the chapter "The Concept of Biblical Authority," he made reference to *The Battle for the Bible* which appeared in 1976. Then he mentioned the book *Biblical Authority* which included a series of articles defending Fuller Theological Seminary. He wrote: "In 1977 Paul Rees, Jack Rogers (editor), Clark Pinnock (a peculiar exception), Berkeley Mickelsen, Bernard Ramm, and David Hubbard published a book, *Biblical Authority,* with the purpose of defending an erroneous Bible. Obviously their concept of authority differs from that of historical evangelicalism, for it is hard to see how falsehood can be authoritative." Note here how Dr. Clark applauds Clark Pinnock as one who then believed in biblical inerrancy. His main point was to find a definition for the word "authority."

Clark said that Berkeley Mickelsen came as close as any to defining that term in his chapter in the book titled "The Bible's Own Approach to Authority." But he thought it was not done adequately and added: "What the book needs is a definition of Biblical authority, for this omission leaves the reader wondering how a book containing errors can be authoritative. Among the examples Mickelsen gives, he did not list the right to tell falsehoods. But if, as these authors assert, the Bible is not inerrant, either it is not God's Word, or God has the authority to tell us what is not so . . . . [The authors of this book] never show how falsehoods can be authoritative" (p. 128). This passage illustrates the use of

Clarkean logic at its best. He simply refuses to let people make assertions that defy logic or denigrate the Word of God. He is wholly the logician when he said, "And can we suppose that the Holy Spirit inspired his prophets to tell lies?"

In his defense of the Word of God Dr. Clark does use a variety of rhetorical methods even as the Bible does. There is some sarcasm, some hyperbole for effect, some asking of questions for effect with no answer expected, and many others. These tend to sharpen his witness, make clear his points, and force the reader to give serious attention to his main arguments. Clark the scholar can reach down to the literate and illiterate as when he wrote: "Ask any Georgia cracker, any Indiana Hoosier, any northwest lumberjack, any graduate of Vassar or Bryn Mawr, would they answer that 'The Bible is free from error in the whole and in the part' means it contains historical, chronological, and geographical falsehoods?" Gordon Clark indeed used the best of literary conventions to make his points.

Gordon Clark was quite gentlemanly when dealing with those he was in disagreement with. We have already mentioned how he carefully exempted Pinnock from identification with those who at the time of the writing were saying the Bible has errors in it. He was also quite appreciative of Bernard Ramm with whom he had substantial differences over Ramm's notion that evangelical orthodoxy had no leg to stand on apart from the work and views of Karl Barth. He reviewed Dr. Ramm's book in the *Fundamentalist Journal (After Fundamentalism: The Future of Evangelical Theology,* Harper and Row, 1982). He said: "Now, this might give the impression that I have a grudge against Ramm. On the contrary, our contacts, while disappointingly infrequent across the years, have always been most friendly. I wish to thank him for his kind words about me in this very volume. But it happens that I am as much opposed to Barth as he is favorable . . . ." And he ended his review by saying "I do not thus criticize Ramm in anger, envy, or in academic triumph, but in deep sadness. Ramm is such a fine gentleman. But Christ is sinless" (June 1983 issue, pp. 52, 53). This is the sort of Christian gentleman Gordon Clark was even to those with whom he was in serious disagreement. He made it clear there and elsewhere that theological differences of the most serious nature did not keep him from having ordinary charity as well as respectful relations with non-evangelicals and even pagans.

We turn our attention now from Gordon Haddon Clark the defender of the Christian faith and the firmest advocate of an inerrant Scripture to the Clark of scholarship and academia. He was the author of such fine volumes as *Readings in Ethics*, (1931), *Selections from Hellenistic Philosophy* (1940), *A History of Philosophy* and *Thales to Dewey* (1957), among others. The last named book has been used as a text in many institutions. In it he traces the rise of philosophy from the 7th century B.C. right down to John Dewey the pragmatist and perhaps the most influential educator in the 20th century. Clark displays great learning and superb academic proficiency in this volume. Thus he was both a scholar in the secular sense of that word as well as a Christian scholar who concerned himself with the Christian faith as the only way of salvation. He was a man for all seasons and his interests were diverse. He made it plain a variety of ways that science is, as he said, "always false." And he provided the rationale for this statement that no one yet has been able to gainsay. This brings us to the personal life of a scholar and a defender of the true faith.

A man is to be judged, not on the basis of a single attribute but upon the totality of his life. All have warts and bumps. No one is yet perfect, and Gordon Haddon Clark the Calvinist strongly believed that only upon glorification is the believer made perfect and sinless, truly shaped in the image of the Creator's intention as Adam and Eve were fashioned and as they lived before the fall. What was lost in the fall is regained for the Christian at last when he is glorified at death. No one, least of all Dr. Clark, would have claimed perfection in this life, and he was acutely aware of his own condition. But this does not mean that he had no noble and useful characteristics.

Gordon Clark was a man of integrity. He was uncompromising in what he believed, taught, and practiced. He was consistent in his life style modelled after his biblical world and life view. He was a fine husband and father. He was an honest man who did not conceal what he believed and thus was frank in his conversation. He called a spade a spade. Yet he never gave the appearance of anger nor was he nasty, harsh, or brutal. He was hospitable in heart and home and enjoyed many friendships with people of opposing viewpoints. At the same time it must be said that he did alienate people. And this must be explained in the proper context.

Those who disliked Gordon Clark did so because of his theology, not for his person. Their dislike may have caused them to be critical of his person as well. But it was really his theology that lay at the center of their feelings. There can be no doubt that the kind of Calvinism Clark represented is difficult to accept but that is not the real issue. The basic question is whether the viewpoint he espoused can be sustained from Scripture. And once logic is accepted, a logic employed even by those who detested his viewpoint,

Clark stands tall and his case is yet to be shown to be wrong. What I have in mind here can be demonstrated by the remark made by Clark Pinnock that I have already mentioned.

Pinnock referred to Clark's "weird combination of pure rationalism [sic] dark predestinarian ruminations." Why the writings of Clark should be labelled "weird," or "dark" is not explained by Professor Pinnock. But such words do have implications about the personhood of the individual who is under discussion. And when Dr. Pinnock uses the phrase "No such luck" he is making plain what the real difference is between himself and Dr. Clark. Dr. Clark did not believe in "luck" in any sense of the term. And the belief or disbelief in luck is the line that marks the theological gulf that will always separate those who believe in God's sovereignty and those who don't. There is one other aspect to this sad business that should not be overlooked. I doubt that Dr. Clark did or ever would use words like "weird" and "dark" with regard to Dr. Pinnock's theological convictions and system. He would surely say they are incorrect and he would fight them passionately, but he would do so in a gentlemanly fashion.

I think Dr. Pinnock is quite wrong when he says that God is not wholly omniscient. I think the implications of such a statement are unfortunate. They attack the truth claims of the Word of God. And if Dr. Pinnock had departed this life I would surely not say that I hoped that Dr. Pinnock would have rested in peace and that we would have some relief from his weird combination of irrational, unbiblical, anti-predestinarian, speculative ruminations! Rather I would speak well of him as a Christian and a scholar and be grateful that he has openly spoken about his views so that the Christian public can note the differences between them and historic orthodoxy and carry on a dialogue by which people like myself might seek to get Pinnock to change his views were he alive and well. I am grateful that William Barclay wrote his autobiography and that the Eerdman's company published it. Barclay openly stated that he was a universalist, that Jesus is not God, that a vicarious atonement is not biblical, and that the virgin birth of Jesus Christ is untrue. Thus those who have read and widely used his New Testament commentary series and supposed that he stood in the tradition of orthodoxy would know the truth and act accordingly.

I think that Gordon Haddon Clark would agree that it is important for evangelical Christians to have available the works of those who are the worst enemies of the Christian faith—such as Dewey, Gibbon, Paine, Hume, Voltaire, and Diderot. Only then can the Christian evaluate what the opponents of Christianity are thinking and saying. And only then can they create an apologetic in the defense of the Christian faith, the Bible, and traditional orthodoxy.

Dr. Clark is dead. But he has left behind him a series of scholarly works that have significant value for those who embrace historic orthodoxy. They may not agree with every detail of what he has written but at least they will know what this giant stood for and on what basis he did this. He has also left behind him a number of able and articulate spokesmen to carry on the work he engaged in so passionately while on earth. Alive or dead he must be reckoned with, even as we continue to reckon with John Calvin and Augustine. Those who knew Dr. Clark personally have good reason to thank God that he ordained this man from eternity past to be a spokesman for His glory, for the good of men and for the advancement of God's eternal kingdom!

Clark and Contemporary Thought

Ronald Nash

Gordon Clark was one of the premier Christian thinkers of the twentieth century. Few Christian thinkers defended the cause of biblical Christianity with as much determination and as much skill as Clark. It is important to remember that much of Clark's important work occurred during the deep theological valley that marked the lowest point in the fortunes of American fundamentalism. It is also important to note that evangelicalism was led out of that pit largely through the efforts of Clark and two of his philosophy students at Wheaton College, Carl Henry and E.J. Carnell. From the year when J. Gresham Machen died (1937) to the first publications of Henry and Carnell after World War II, Clark stood almost alone for the set of essential beliefs that came to serve as the foundation of evangelical scholarship in the 1950s. Others who may have shared Clark's convictions neglected the vital matter of getting those views into print.

Clark's influence came first through his teaching the rather remarkable group of young evangelicals who attended his philosophy classes at Wheaton College in the years just prior to the start of World War II. Carl Henry has provided an interesting account of what it must have been like to study under Clark in the setting.*

Clark's service at Wheaton was then shamefully terminated by a board and president in an act all too typical of the short-sightedness and shallowness of fundamentalism. After Clark secured another teaching position, this time at Butler University in Indianapolis, his major influence had to come through his publications. When I first began to teach the history of philosophy at Barrington College in the late 1950s, I used Clark's *Thales To Dewey, A Christian View of Men and Things,* and *Religion, Reason and Revelation* as three books that properly prepared evangelicals ought to study.

My own debt to Gordon Clark is incalculable. Unfortunately, I never had the opportunity to know him as a teacher. In fact, I only met Clark twice—once at a meeting of the Evangelical Theological Society in Nashville and once at Covenant College where we had dinner together. But I have always regarded myself as one of his students. At that important stage of my life when I began sharpening my teeth on philosophy and theology, his writings gave me a foundation that I've been able to build on over the years.

Clark played the role of tutor with regard to several of my own books. Clark's expertise in ancient philosophy, especially in the area of the thought of the pagan Plotinus and the Christian Augustine, was well-known. Hence, when I was working on the manuscript that became my book, *The Light of the Mind: St. Augustine's Theory of Knowledge,* I benefited enormously from Clark's detailed comments on an early draft. That book challenged the standard Roman Catholic interpretations of Augustine's illumination theory and correctly, I believe, pointed to a more adequate

---

* See Carl F.H. Henry, *Confessions of a Theologian* (Waco: Word, 1986).

interpretation of Augustine's position. The Augustine of that book was clearly a forerunner of the kind of position Clark came to defend so eloquently in our own century.

To the best of my recollection, I did not ask Clark for comments on the manuscript of what became my eighth book, *The Word of God and the Mind of Man*. But my debt in that book to Clark's earlier work should be obvious to any knowledgeable reader. That book clearly builds on the foundation Clark had already laid and unmasks the absurdity of the neo-orthodox repudiation of propositional revelation and the irrationalism of evangelicals like Cornelius Van Til, Herman Dooyeweerd, and others.

Sometime during 1983—after he had moved to Covenant College—I did ask Clark to review the manuscript for what became my book, *Christianity and the Hellenistic World*. Even though Clark was then in his eighties, his mind was as sharp as ever. His corrections and suggestions, done from memory, did much to improve the book.

There is much that contemporary philosophers and theologians ought to have learned from Clark: (1) the epistemological bankruptcy of any form of philosophical or religious empiricism;* (2) the indispensability of Divine revelation to human knowledge as a whole;† (3) the shortcomings of any attempt to remove the cognitive and propositional element from the content of God's revelation;‡ (4) the importance of refusing to separate faith from reason whether this separation be a humanistic attack on faith, an existentialist critique of reason, or a Thomistic

---

* For my statement of this position, see *The Word of God and the Mind of Man*, chapter 7.
† For one of my statements on this matter, see Ronald Nash, *Faith and Reason: Searching for a Rational Faith* (Grand Rapids: Zondervan, 1988).
‡ For more on this, see *The Word of God and the Mind of Man*.

segregation of the two into different realms of human knowledge;* (5) the continuing vitality and relevance of Calvinistic theology as formulated, for example, in The Westminster Confession.

It is tragic that contemporary evangelical scholars are in the process of forgetting Clark's important work. A number of evangelical seminaries have opened the door and welcomed a Barthian-like irrationalism that attempts to distinguish human reason and logic from divine reason.† Clark was correct when he warned that down this path lies nothing but skepticism. Basic to the Christian worldview, Clark insisted, is the presupposition that human beings are the image of God. Essential to this image is a rationality that reflects the rationality of God's own mind. The *Logos* teaching of the New Testament and the early church fathers entails a similarity between the rational structure of the human mind and the rational structure of the divine mind. It is possible for the human *logos* to know the divine *Logos* because God created humans as creatures who have the God-given ability to know the divine mind and to think God's thoughts after Him. The laws of reason are the same for both God and man.

One of the most unfortunate features of contemporary theology is a turning away from any objective, fixed reference points in religion that can serve as guides to inward religious experience and serve as tests of false inward religious experience. There is nothing in the nature of divine transcendence that precludes the possibility of

---

* One place where I defend this at length is my book, *Christian Faith and Historical Understanding* (Grand Rapids: Zondervan, 1984).

† Ironically, Cornelius Van Til of Westminster Seminary was very close to Barth on this position. See chapter 9 of *The Word of God and the Mind of Man*.

our knowing the mind of God. There is nothing irrational or illogical about the content of divine revelation. The Christian God is not the Unknown God of ancient Athens or of modern Marburg. He is a God who created men and women as creatures capable of knowing his mind and will; He is a God who has made information about His mind and will available in revealed truths.*

Gordon Clark is perhaps the dean of those twentieth century American philosophers who sought to develop a Christian worldview consistent with the Christian Scriptures. There are fads in philosophy, of course, and Clark's views are not popular in this day. But as one of Clark's former students, Edward John Carnell, once put it: "Truth can never be discovered by counting noses." I for one am convinced that Clark set forth views that must be part and parcel of any adequate Christian philosophy.

Anyone today who works through Clark's writings will recognize the mind of a man whose devotion to truth and wisdom is not one whit less than his devotion to the triune God. And this is as it should be, for Clark carried with him the Augustinian conviction that to know the truth is to know God since God is truth. The contributors to this book can only talk about Clark and invite others to explore his writings for themselves. Readers of this book who accept the challenge and turn next to the actual writings of Gordon Clark will find an enriching experience awaiting them.

* See Ronald Nash, "Southern Baptists and the Notion of Revealed Truth," *Criswell Theological Review*, Vol. 2 (1988), pp. 371-384.

Valiant-for-Truth

Joseph Pattison, M.D.

Like many others I have held Gordon Clark in the highest esteem, for many reasons, but chiefly in my own case, because in the providence of the Most High God I was brought to repentance and saving faith under his tutelage. It was many years ago but hardly a month goes by that I do not recall with thanksgiving his series on our Reformation heritage, framed in the context of the Five Points of Calvinism and presented to a small number of attendees on five successive Sunday evenings in a small Presbyterian church in Indianapolis in November 1953 (Dr. William Young was one of us). I was transfixed by the clarity of the presentation, the comprehensive Biblical emphasis, the sustained logical ordering of Christian doctrines, and by his faithfulness to Christianity in its most comprehensive statement. There was no coercive insistence that any one make up his mind at the moment, no appeal to "experience," or to examples, no antics, only a total devotion to and reliance on the irresistible grace of God, who works when, where, and how He pleases. The focus was ever on the Triune God and the Word. He was one of the most spiritual and faithful Christians I have been privileged to know, certainly the most influential in my life. He was

Valiant-for-Truth, always steadfast in the proclamation of the Reformed faith amidst the welter of conflicting and heretical fashions.

He was often a man of few words. His reply to a remark might be a "So?", which could be quite disconcerting. Perhaps he was inviting me to draw a conclusion, or to further define my position or intent. Usually I would change the subject.

Dr. and Mrs. Clark were gracious and entertaining hosts when my wife and I would visit them on our return trips to Indiana. Ruth was his "memory and factotum" (his words). After her death in 1977, Louise and I would have him out for dinner with our younger children when we were visiting Covenant College on Lookout Mountain. He was a delightful guest, with clever and humorous remarks. I think he was especially appreciative of the children's presence. He would never ignore them.

And one last fond remembrance: When I proposed to my wife-to-be, her parents were still in the Belgian Congo (where they were missionaries for many years). It was therefore incumbent upon me to plead my cause by mail. Dr. Cousar's response was favorable, thanks be to God. He, too, was appreciative of Clark's writings, and so one thing that recommended me to him was my enthusiasm for his contributions.

His life was an enduring influence upholding the glory of God and the Word of God; and providing direction and encouragement to many, *e.g.,* in catechizing our children in the rudiments of the faith, I was often reminded of his example.

How You Can Meet Gordon Clark

John W. Robbins*

I met Gordon Clark reading a book: *Religion, Reason and Revelation.* I don't recall the exact year—probably 1970, but it may have been a year later.

As a graduate student in political theory and philosophy at The Johns Hopkins University, I knew that I would have to write a defensible doctoral dissertation. Therefore, I began looking for a defensible philosophy. I read Thomas Aquinas, C.S. Lewis, and Francis Schaeffer, among others, but I decided that their systems were not defensible. It was too easy to find the flaws in their arguments for the existence of God, and if those arguments fail, the whole Thomistic system collapses.

In high school and college I had read R.J. Rushdoony, for he wrote about subjects that interested me: politics, education, and American history. Since he thought highly of Cornelius Van Til, I read everything by Van Til that I could find. This meant semi-annual trips to Nutley, New Jersey, stopping by 55 Beech Street to pick up Charles Craig, then a man in his sixties, driving over to his warehouse and selecting a large box or two of books at half

*President, The Trinity Foundation

price—Oswald Allis, B.B. Warfield, J. Gresham Machen, Herman Dooyeweerd, R.J. Rushdoony, as well as Cornelius Van Til—whatever Mr. Craig sold, I bought.

None of the authors I read mentioned Clark very favorably. Some had written before Clark's time; others ignored him; a few made disparaging remarks. As a result, Clark's were the last of the books to be read. But, as Scripture says, sometimes the last are first.

Clark's essay on "God and Evil" in *Religion, Reason, and Revelation* convinced me that here was a man who offered what I was looking for: a defensible philosophy. He tackled one of the most important problems of Christian philosophy, the problem of evil, and dealt with it candidly, honestly, logically, and Biblically. There was no rhetorical backing and filling, no pious platitudes about God "permitting" bad things to happen, no desire to ignore the problem and hope it will go away. I found in that book, in contrast to most other books written by professed Calvinists, a willingness to believe the statements of Scripture and a rapier sharp intellect wielded in defense of revealed truth. I immediately began reading all the rest of Clark's work, and I learned more and more about him, and through him, about Christ.

It wasn't for several more years that I actually shook Gordon Clark's hand. After that meeting, I realized that his books sound like his voice: deep, well-modulated, witty, deliberate, thoughtful. Even today, as any of his students can attest, one can pick up his books and "hear" him speaking.

In February 1978 our third daughter was born, and we made arrangements to have Clark baptize her at the church he attended in Lookout Mountain. Three of us flew to Chattanooga one Saturday in May, met Clark at church on

Sunday morning, and he took us out to dinner that afternoon. In the evening he baptized Mary Ellen Robbins.

The next day he gave us a guided tour of the Civil War battlefields around Lookout Mountain, and we were amazed that a man of 75 years could walk as far and as fast as he did. More amazing still was his knowledge of the War; he gave detailed descriptions of armies, commanders, troop movements, and engagements. One might have thought that American history, not ancient philosophy, was his field.

During this trip I told Clark that some relatives, friends, and I had just established a Foundation to publish essays and books. He asked, which books? I told him his. He looked startled at first, but as we discussed the plan, he seemed to think that it was a good idea. Before we left, he insisted on giving me a generous check to help get Trinity into business.

From about 1973 to 1985 Clark and I corresponded. I remember asking him in late 1972 or early 1973 where I should apply for a teaching job. He advised me not to seek a job at a religious college, for I would be afforded more freedom to teach and write at a private secular school. I presumed then that he was recalling his unfortunate experience at Wheaton College in Illinois, which, even 45 years ago, disliked the doctrines of grace.

It was not for another five years that I saw Clark again, this time in Colorado, where he taught during the summer. The years between had been filled with correspondence, telephone calls, and several newly published Clark books and essays. I sat in his classes for only two summers, 1983 and 1984, and saw him for the last time on Earth in October 1984. He was an extraordinary man. In the providence of

God, when this student needed help, Clark was there, talking about God and evil, logic and knowledge, time and eternity. It is my hope that what I received through Clark—a thoroughly defensible philosophy—others may find as well.

Clark no longer confines his lectures to the mountains of Colorado, the plains of Indiana, and the hills of Georgia. His classes are much larger now, and they are offered all over the globe. Those who have not met him may regret it, but don't regret it too much. New acquaintances will be made, as well as old acquaintances renewed, in Heaven, which is only—at most—a few years away for any Christian. But if you would like to know Clark now, it is not too late. There are more Clark books in print in 1989 than there were at any time while he lived among us. If you wish to meet the man, read his books.

A Truly Great and Brilliant Friend

Robert K. Rudolph*

My father, the late Bishop Robert L. Rudolph, who was also professor from 1906 to 1930 at the Reformed Episcopal Seminary, first introduced me to Gordon Clark, probably in my freshman year at the University of Pennsylvania. Gordon was seeking to organize a branch of the League of Evangelical Students at Penn and, of course, I was eager to help (especially under my dad's urging).

Clark had become acquainted with Father while our Southern Jurisdiction in South Carolina was under him as Presiding Bishop. My father was responsible for our Bishop Stevens Seminary in Summerville, South Carolina. The teaching was done by Lutheran and Presbyterian ministers who volunteered their services for the time. My dad looked for a good theology textbook and discovered the one written by Dr. Clark's father which was so clear and plain for our Negroes of that day. The jurisdiction had then from 25 to 30 churches and the Seminary had, perhaps, 15 students from many denominations, but, of course, quite a

*Former Professor, Reformed Episcopal Seminary, Philadelphia, Pennsylvania

few of our own black young men.

My father bought quite a quantity of Dr. David S. Clark's textbooks. He paid for them and provided them. So Dr. David Clark asked Gordon to look up this Bishop Rudolph who was buying almost all of his stock of books. Dr. David Clark wrote the book basically for a school up on the "boulevard" in which he had been teaching. (I do not know the name of the school.) Gordon lived with his parents on North 19th St. about a block from Dr. Clark's church. He was an instructor at Penn in the philosophy department under the late Dr. William Romaine Newbold. Gordon Clark had a book in which was inscribed "To Gordon Haddon Clark in whose mind the mind of William Romaine Newbold took much delight." Among other courses that Gordon taught was one that had been taught for years by Dr. Newbold, a history of the philosophy of Christianity—essentially a delineation of the doctrinal development of Christianity especially as brought out by the rise of heresy and its downfall as believers studied God's Word. After the death of Dr. Newbold everyone expected Gordon to become the head of the department as Dr. Newbold clearly desired.

But it was about the time when the Presbyterian conflict rose toward its crescendo. There was a very powerful and controlling man at Penn who had much to say about faculty appointments, but he was a liberal in the U.S.A. Church, and he told Gordon that he would never get the appointment since he was such a troublemaker in the Church. Gordon had left the old Church and later was ordained as a teaching elder in the Orthodox Presbyterian Church. He had been ordained as a ruling elder in the U.S.A. Church. In the Orthodox Presbyterian Church he was opposed by Dr. Cornelius Van Til's great opposition to the old apologetics of the Church. Van Til felt that the "systematic consistency" test for truth had led them into compromise with unbelief and insisted upon a "Systemic" but not propositional definition of truth. He really loved Gordon Clark dearly (Clark assured me of his feeling that the opposition was *not* personal, that Van Til loved him very much)—but he feared that the "old" apologetics which had destroyed the Church, if not replaced by his suggested "Presuppositional Thinking," would work around again to the same destruction.

When the Orthodox Presbyterian Church was formed and Gordon joined, his father did not see the necessity of another church. Father and son loved each other greatly, and the hurt for them both at having to follow different courses was keen and deep. Of course the love persisted, but the division hurt the more thereby.

***

I offered to install one of the new RCA electric powered radios for Dr. and Mrs. David Clark and spent a few days getting an effective antenna on the roof and wiring it all up. I had some time to talk with Gordon's mother.

She told me with some pride of Gordon's being very precocious. He finished high school with very high grades (*I think* it was at 17). At the University of Pennsylvania he had earned the Ph.D. by the time he was 27. He had majored in philosophy under Newbold. Dr. Newbold was of an old Philadelphia family and was a devout and sincere believer in the Bible. He was a Protestant Episcopalian.

Mrs. Clark also told me of Gordon's unbelievable thoroughness and fast reading and how as a boy he had read every theology book in Dr. David Clark's library and discussed matters often with his father. She also said how such thoroughness had once given her a terrific shock.

Gordon became interested in "mesmerism" (I cannot think of the better name). He had read through all the books he could lay his hands on in the main library. Then one day he had brought a friend of his home, and he put him under such a spell that the boy could not be brought out of his trance. Much to her horror, Mrs. Clark had to call the boy's mother up and tell her of the circumstances and with many apologies reported that since Gordon could not get him out of the trance, she had called the doctor who informed her to let the boy sleep through the night and that he would wake up back to normal. It was done and the result was as the doctor had asserted. She told me how Gordon became completely fearful of such power and never tried to use it in any way again!

Mrs. Clark was of the Haddon family (the Victor Talking Machine family) and had, I think, some small inheritance. It must have been about 1929 that Gordon married Ruth Schmidt, whose parents opposed the affair as much as they could. Ruth, of course, had a degree in botany from Penn. I am not sure when Mrs. Clark died, but it must have been around 1929. *[It was in 1930.—Editor]* Dear old Dr. Clark was still pastor of his church and wanted to continue but could not keep the house by himself and did not want to impose himself on Gordon's new marriage. He knew of a younger woman, Helen Canning, who was a trained nurse by profession and a graduate of the Deaconness School where Dr. Clark taught; he married her and she was the new Mrs. Clark while he lived. When he died, Gordon and Ruth took care of her up here in this wonderful Quarryville Presbyterian Home. She lived here quite a few years until she too died. They always spoke to and of her as "Mrs. Clark."

In 1930 we invited Gordon and Ruth to spend the

summer with us using our guest apartment in Dorset, Vermont. It was that summer that Gordon left the family in Dorset and went to the Boston area to go over the manuscript of Carnell's first apologetics book. By the time of the second book, he parted company with Carnell for abandoning the faith.

As I was taking courses at Penn and at Westminster, I would often go from a class with Van Til to a class with Gordon and *vice versa*. It did enable me to ask questions of both in rather quick succession. Of course, I was not in the class of either because of my thinking ability or "scholarship." I loved them both dearly and could only wish that there had been some way to reconcile them, the one to the other. Deep down I had the conviction that basically they were really not far apart but each insisted on certain assertions that the other could not make.

Gordon was absolutely insistent that we did know some of the same things that God knew. If not, he insisted, it would be impossible for us to know *any* truth at all! That 2 plus 2 equals 4 is true, he felt. Thus he insisted that in and of itself it is *true* as a statement without the necessity of examining another proposition. He carefully insisted upon a propositional concept of truth while Van Til insisted upon the fact that to have truth in one's mind that mind must build upon other propositions. The truthfulness or falsity demanded that the individual proposition be held in the midst of certain other basic propositions that must be consciously present in that mind in order to correctly know truth. Now, of course, God knows every proposition in the context of *all other* propositions for Van Til, and, therefore, the limited human mind *never* knows it the way God does. Van Til had an expression, oft repeated: "true as far as it goes," meaning, of course, that for *that* mind which holds all propositions in a *system*, the more complete the system, the more full the truth. With growth in the knowledge of basic propositions, the further that mind had the truth. Van Til's concept is that for relative human beings, they can have all needful truth but never perceive it as God does with his infinite knowledge of everything that affects any proposition. He charged Clark, therefore, with denying the incomprehensibility of God and Clark charged him with agnosticism since he thought that for him it was impossible to know anything as God did. Clark wanted an absolute even if it were only in the single proposition.

To go back a way earlier, my father saw the tremendous ability of Gordon to think and teach. Dr. Van Til said that Clark was probably the most effective teacher he knew and that therefore he was afraid of the great influence he would have on students and that Clark's effectiveness would do much harm—more so than most other men.

So before my father's death in 1930 and afterwards for quite a while—probably until Gordon left Penn and went to Wheaton—he taught at our Seminary. Many of our students came from Bible School (not college then) and often felt that they knew all there was to be known. They would oppose Gordon, who, with his excellent Socratic method, would soon bring them into a frame of mind where they could learn! These clashes would usually center around being a thorough Calvinist, which Gordon was. Since he was himself a pre-mil believer, that did not bring so much clash. Of course his position was carefully undergirded with Scripture, and so he did clash with some of the excesses of their system.

I was sorry when Clark went to Wheaton as I felt I knew the approach there and that Gordon would run afoul of their prejudices. He certainly did! He and Dr. Buswell were quite far apart on so much, and when student complaints against his clear-cut Calvinism ran into the semi-Arminianism generally taught, sparks flew very high —they even reached such a point that when he and Ruth and the children went to church—almost no matter which —he was confronted with them praying for his salvation! It became utterly unendurable, yet Clark was so very right and they were so very wrong, according to the Bible, in their understanding of man as a "free creature," that there was no peace at all.

Clark's call to Butler University, where he was given free rein to run the Philosophy Department and was able often to bring in Westminster men, etc., made for a situation where he could teach the truth without interference.

I have not touched, I think, on the episode of our (I was on the Board with Bishop Higgins and mostly Dutch men —oh how their heavy smoking tried us at the meetings in the little room!) seeking to establish a Christian University. Ed Rian (who had secured the estate for Westminster and worked on its payment) did secure the Weidner estate, and he raised quite a sum of money but finally was not able to raise enough for us to be able to open the doors and pay a faculty. Lacking about $200,000, he suggested that a "Board of Reference," having no control but willing to recommend the institution, be formed on which there could be leading pre-mils and Wheatonians so we could get money from those sources. The Christian Reformed, he pointed out, had their own institutions and he had secured all the help he could from them. In the meantime we had begun to try to choose an opening faculty. Many of us deemed Gordon Clark the right man to head the Philosophy Department, but Dr. Van Til, backed by a number of the others, strongly opposed it for the same reasons he had opposed Gordon's ordination earlier. The financial problem brought it to a halt anyway. Finally, John Murray, backed by a number of others, said that the proposed idea of a "Board of Reference" was not honest since they would certainly expect pre-mil Arminians to be able to partake if they lent their help. He pointed out that what Ed Rian proposed would ultimately destroy the Reformed character of the University. If people from such a large group did substantial giving there would thereafter always be the threat of losing income unless we adopted their position. For him and for many others of us too, the effort was not worth it since there was evidently not enough sentiment to support the truly Reformed Christian University which we envisioned. With that vote the effort was abandoned and the property allowed to go back to the Weidner Estate. The $150,000 given us by Mrs. Rath (of the Rath meat family) thus was lost and the money of not a few others. The Weidner estate, however, deducted much of that amount (which they had already received from Christian sources) from the price finally paid by Carl McIntire's group to purchase Faith Seminary.

To me it was very noticeable that when considering someone not known well to the group—someone from another area, agreement as to their being on the faculty was forthcoming. But practically everyone known to the group rather well had a goodly opposition!

Gordon's clear thinking and quiet presentation, I will never forget and, as a friend, he was very precious indeed.

He loved his studies at the Sorbonne and began to be much more French even in the way he ate!

His absolute self-control and apparent failure to show emotion was, doubtless, the outcome of his conviction that there was no such thing as emotion—only less well-considered attitudes and actions!

I hope some of this may serve your purpose to establish a true remembrance of a truly great and brilliant friend of mine!

A Sense of the Holiness of God

John W. Sanderson*

One of my first impressions of Gordon Clark was that of a man profoundly influenced by a sense of the holiness of God. He was the first in my experience to mention Charnock's volumes on the attributes of God. The first sermon I heard him preach was on Matthew 21:33-44, and I shall always remember that he closed the sermon by repeating the words of verse 41 and then adding his own to the effect, "What a terrifying prospect." Knowing how carefully he chose his words, I was profoundly affected.

The only time I saw him upset, even red-faced, was when he was discussing the transgression of a Christian leader. Normally well-composed, he was shocked at that sin.

Another side to his character was his gentleness. He had a student who worked as a night watchman and frequently slept in class. Dr. Clark never reproved him. On one occasion the student came to the classroom early and promptly fell into a deep sleep. When it was time for class to begin, Dr. Clark called the rest of us to another corner of the room and lectured softly for the hour session. Then he went

*Former Professor, Covenant College and Seminary

over to the sleeping student, and gently said, "You can wake up now."

Once he lectured for a class in Medieval Philosophy at my invitation, and with rapier-like precision he cut down students who wanted to debate with him the merits of empiricism. To say the least, they were embarrassed and chagrined to see their pet arguments so easily punctured. After the class he followed me to my office and asked for the names of the students who had spoken. He wanted to give each of them an autographed copy of one of his books!

As everyone knows, Dr. Clark liked to play chess and could play it with the best of them. One college professor complained to me that he could never get his gambits started—Dr. Clark had already put him in check. Yet rumor has it that he would go to a local Christian school to play with the sixth graders, and he would let them win—sometimes!

Graciousness always characterized his ways with students. He was busy translating Plotinus, writing the translation on leaves which had been inserted into his Greek/French text of that ancient philosopher. To keep his writing small he used a magnifying glass and a very fine point on his pen. He complained that sometimes as he dipped his pen into the ink bottle (this was in the days before ball point pens) he spilled the ink over his desk. Some of us bought him a glass desk set which could not be tipped, and we placed it in his office while he was away. Next day we received the following note: "Therefore with joy I will draw ink from the wells of your kindness."

Dr. Clark wanted us to choose our words and use them correctly. At a dormitory banquet at which he was speaker some wiseacres had prepared the menu using scientific terms for each of the items to be eaten. Thus "peas" were listed by their botanical term. Searching out the committee members, Dr. Clark suggested that the letter "L" should be added to the term, "in the interests of accuracy."

He enjoyed a good joke, and there was usually a glint in his eyes when he was about to say something funny. And he could be very sly about it. One semester we had a course in Aristotle at 3:30 in the afternoon. Aristotle at 3:30! In April of that year, the class conflicted with a baseball game and we knew Dr. Clark enjoyed baseball. So the few students in the class agreed to cut class that day. Instead we gathered in front of his office to meet him when he returned from the empty classroom. We explained that we wanted to go to the game and discuss Aristotle's theory of motion. He agreed, adding that he hoped we had heard the announcement he had just made in the classroom. He had just announced to the empty chairs that there would be a test the following week! It was not an easy test, and we didn't see any more ball games that semester.

But Dr. Clark's major concerns were with the kingdom of God and its advancement. He led a "Creed Club" at Wheaton for students on Sunday afternoons, expounding a chapter of the Westminster Confession each week. Many had their first introduction to Calvinism in such meetings.

He was interested in apologetics and the need for giving a reason for our hope. In those early days the writings of Dr. Cornelius Van Til were becoming known. Dr. Clark used Van Til's mimeographed notes as the basis for one of his courses. Some of us wanted Dr. Buswell's reactions also and persuaded him to offer a seminar on the same notes. We would carry the opinions of one to the other's class, but it was soon clear that we needed a confrontation. It was a great evening for all of us when, late in the semester, we went to the Buswell home to listen to the discussion between these two men. It soon became clear that our two teachers were not to find "common ground."

Dr. Clark had a quiet ministry among his students. I remember hearing a member of the Gospel team say that he knew nothing about Jesus Christ "until I went to the University of Pennsylvania." In philosophy classes under Dr. Clark he had become a Christian and was preparing for a ministry.

In his later years, Dr. Clark became involved in a program in Chattanooga teaching English as a second language. Although he was busy writing, he went with others to teach recent immigrants to read the Bible.

The Proper Use of the Mind

Roland G. Usher, Jr.*

Gordon Clark was an esteemed colleague of mine at Butler University who also was happy to have, with me, an extra-curricular activity of leading adult classes in Great Books. I have always, as a consequence, had a picture of Gordon as banned to a cloud in Cloud Cuckoo Land a la Aristophanes (*The Clouds,* 423 B.C.), and debating with John Calvin and with Archbishop James Ussher the probability of the existence of clouds.

Somewhat less flippantly, and Gordon was never flippant, he always enjoyed debate; and he always enjoyed putting people on. He had a puckish sense of humor which enabled him to trap a poor unsuspecting adult in a philosophical oddity from which there was no escape. Philosophy being his business, of course, this was always his game; and he enjoyed nothing more than leading the unsuspecting on step by step into a horrendous Pandora's Box of illogical consequences.

With Gordon, of course, clearing the mind and training it in the logic of good thought was what it was all about. He devoted himself to finding the truth as mercilessly as any

*Professor Emeritus of History, Butler University, Indianapolis, Indiana

historian might do, but for him the end was not in the proper construct to which laboriously gathered parts might lead, but rather in the golden rule of the proper use of the mind as a God-given instrument. Gordon was always reverent.

Absolute Truth

William Young*

While I was an undergraduate at Columbia College in New York, I became acquainted with the League of Evangelical Students, and a chapter was formed on the campus. The advising board in 1931 consisted of Melvin Grove Kyle, Leander S. Keyser, J. Gresham Machen, Clarence Bouma and Harold Paul Sloan. In 1938 there were over 70 chapters in Christian and secular institutions of higher learning. On the program for the first summer conference in 1936 is listed Studies in Romans by Gordon H. Clark, Ph.D., Philosophy Department, University of Pennsylvania.

I was also acquainted with some of Dr. Clark's writing when I was an undergraduate, active in the League of Evangelical Students of which he was an enthusiastic supporter. At Westminster Seminary in the year 1939-40, I recall that the junior class, including President Clowney, was overwhelmingly the result of Dr. Clark's Creed Club and Calvinistic teaching at Wheaton College.

The Creed Club, I understand, was an informal group

*Chairman, Department of Philosophy, University of Rhode Island, Barrington.

of students in which the Westminster Confession of Faith was studied, and a number of the Wheaton students became Calvinists. While Dr. Clark was on excellent terms with J. Oliver Buswell, the president of Wheaton when he was hired, his teaching of Calvinism and, in particular, his criticism of emotionalism in religion proved to be alien to the outlook of Dr. Buswell's successor; and Dr. Clark was obliged to leave Wheaton. While in 1938-41 Dr. Van Til referred critically to Dr. Clark's views on the incomprehensibility of God and the place of the emotions, yet no one dreamed of bringing charges of heresy against a stalwart champion for the faith.

In the controversy over the *Complaint* against Philadelphia Presbytery of the Orthodox Presbyterian Church for ordaining Dr. Clark to the preaching ministry, at first Dr. Van Til's authority weighed heavily with me, as with others in the Orthodox Presbyterian Church. I was away from the scene in Toronto 1944-46, but at the General Assembly of the Orthodox Presbyterian Church when Dr. Clark was subjected to elaborate questioning, I was convinced by his answers that he believed in total depravity and that the allegations of heresy were unfounded. I was elected to the committee to study the doctrines of the *Complaint,* and concurred with Floyd Hamilton on the subjects of the noetic effects of sin and the free offer of the Gospel. On the latter point, I presented a "minority" report with which half of the committee agreed.

I taught at Butler University as Dr. Clark's junior colleague from 1947 to 1954. I learned more philosophy from association with him then than at Columbia College or Westminster and Union Seminaries, although I owe much to the eminent thinkers at all three institutions.

I profited from Dr. Clark's lectures but also from

discussions with him. Once I fallaciously argued that since we can talk about "nothing," there must be such a thing. I recall that he used the pseudo-syllogism to the contrary: Half a loaf is better than nothing, and nothing is better than a Thanksgiving dinner; therefore, half a loaf is better than a Thanksgiving dinner.

Once at a luncheon, he was pointing out that there is a one-to-one correspondence between the members of the series of even integers and all the integers, and concluded that there was only one infinity. I mentioned Cantor's diagonal proof that the number of decimals between 0 and 1 is an infinity larger than can be brought into such a correspondence with the integers. Clark replied: "I am silenced, but not convinced."

When in Amsterdam, Dr. Clark had an interview with Dooyeweerd, in which he asked whether there was absolute truth. Dooyeweerd replied in the negative. Clark wrote on a piece of paper: "There is no absolute truth," handed it to Dooyeweerd and asked: "Is what is written absolute truth?"

I inquired, "What did Dooyeweerd say?" I was told this was the wrong question. I should have asked, "What did Dooyeweerd do?" and the answer was, "He smiled."

Since I left Butler, I have kept in touch with the Clarks. Dr. Clark and I had a somewhat extensive correspondence on saving faith. He has been so kind as to review my early book *Toward a Reformed Philosophy* in the *Journal of Philosophy* and to recommend my *Foundations of Theory* and *Hegel's Dialectic* to the Presbyterian and Reformed Publishing Company.

Among other items too numerous to mention, I owe to Dr. Clark some understanding of the importance of logic in philosophy and theology, of the *a priori* in epistemology and the primacy of the intellect. I trust that his emphasis on such matters will exert a permanent influence on the thinking and action of those who profess Evangelical Christianity and the Reformed Faith.

"Cordially, G.H.C."

Dwight F. Zeller

"Cordially, G.H.C." That is the closing which I received on correspondence for twenty-nine years. There was not a large volume of letters from my father-in-law, but through the years when he did write, it was always the same—"Cordially, G.H.C." One might criticize that closing from one's father-in-law, but how many fathers-in-law even write to their daughter's husband? There were several letters like this each year, and usually they demanded an answer or were in answer to something which I had written to him.

Some might even think that this means that through twenty-nine years G.H.C.'s relation to me was always the same. I recall Mother Clark one time mentioning that Dad Clark had always held to the same basic theological position throughout his life while many others changed. That is true, but I cannot say the same thing about his relationship to me. There were changes and developments.

Where shall I start? There are several points at which I could commence with our relationship. The best place is probably chronological, so I will go with that. My parents were friends of the Clarks. Not close friends, but acquainted. My father and Dad Clark were both ministers in the same presbytery of the old United Presbyterian Church in central Indiana. My father had a rural church north of Indianapolis where Dr. Clark would sometimes fill the pulpit. It was during the summer of 1953 while I was taking summer courses at Butler Graduate School of Religion that I met the Clarks. At the same time my mother was taking a course in the undergraduate school to update her teaching certificate. We stopped several times at the Clarks, who lived about two blocks from the campus. Since my folks had a large garden they would give them some fresh produce. Mrs. Clark was a very friendly person who was always gracious, and a person with whom one could easily be friendly. Dr. Clark impressed me as being somewhat aloof, but one who took time from his thinking and studies to be sociable. My future wife was not home that summer, as she was in the Black Hills of South Dakota, studying at the Wheaton College Science Station. I did meet Betsy, the Clarks' junior high daughter, who was sharp and ambitious. I even took a walk or two with her while she collected pop bottles on the Butler campus. She would take them to a grocery store to get the deposit money. I heard they had a college age daughter who was away, so I put that bit of information into my "software," but did nothing about it at that time.

Over a year later, after I had finished seminary and become a chaplain in the Navy, but serving with the Marines, I received a very nice letter from Mrs. Clark. She was a great letter writer, and thought it her duty to write to men in the service. She had gotten my address from my parents. Upon receipt of her letter my "software" information came up on the screen, and I mentioned in my return letter that I would be glad to correspond with one of the girls. About two weeks later I received a very nice letter from the older girl who was a junior at Butler University. This correspondence continued for about two years. The first time we met was several months after that first letter when I was on leave. On my first date with Lois we drove to downtown Indianapolis for something at a Bible Book Store, but when we returned to the car it was GONE! We had parked in a spot where the parking hours were restricted and my car had been towed away. After locating the car and paying the fine we returned to the Clarks; Dr. Clark was most apologetic for the mishap and for the first time I met Dr. Clark, a person who was concerned for others.

It cannot be said that G.H.C. was altogether pleased with my courtship of his daughter. He did not say much to me, but he did to Lois. He had plans for her. She was to finish college then go to France and study there in a Bible Institute. At this point I should say that Lois and I saw little of each other during our courtship of two years. We had about three or four dates, and did the rest by correspondence. The second year of our courtship I was in the Far East on duty. It was during that time that our correspondence became serious and we tentatively decided to get married, but G.H.C. was not happy about having his plans for his daughter interrupted; but he was wise enough to leave the final decision up to her, and when she decided to get married instead of going to France, he did accept it.

Something else should be inserted here. No one needs to be told that Dr. Clark was a superb writer. In the training of his children he insisted that they write effectively. During that two-year correspondence course I had with his daughter, I really came to know her by what she wrote. She could express herself much better with the pen than orally.

From the time of our marriage on, I can somewhat trace my relationship with G.H.C. by how he influenced my reading. I had probably been married to Lois for five to eight years before Dad Clark and I spoke about theology. It appeared to me, and still does, that at that point he was suspicious of my theology. He may have had some good reasons to be, but it was not so much a matter of my position, as it was of the place I was in the development of a mature theological position. Anyway, before we were married he started sending me good books to read. The first was Jewett's *Emil Brunner's Concept of Revelation*. Then he started on Machen's simple apologetics—*What Is Faith, The Christian View of Man,* etc. As I look back, I can see that he had a plan. The first part of this plan was to counteract the Neo-orthodoxy which I had studied—but never accepted —in seminary. The second aspect of this plan was to have me read books by persons other than himself. He understood that the relationship of son-in-law with father-in-law was different from that of others and he went easy with me to make sure that it was a good relationship and that he would have an influence on me.

As the years passed he continued to "feed" me books, and I was greatly influenced by them. But this "feeding" decreased. I do not think that he gave up on me, but it appears that he saw some of his objectives fulfilled, so he did not see the need of "educating" his son-in-law as much as he had before. The letters still read "Cordially G.H.C.", but it even sounded different and said something different after ten or fifteen years.

This situation with books even took a different twist during the last ten to twelve years of his life. As I studied and took more courses in Greek, I would come across new books on the subject and would buy an extra copy for him as Christmas presents. These he was very glad to get and would often use them in his writings. This is not to say that I always agreed with his position on grammar, textual criticism or exegetical issues, but it was a point of contact in which we were both very interested.

After we did start to converse about theology, it seemed to be with reluctance that he did so. I would almost have to force him to answer direct questions. It wasn't that he did not have an interest in my theology, but he wanted to protect a relationship as well as encourage me in the right direction theologically. Of course, when we did talk, he often gave his well-known answer to a question. "Well, you should read _____, and _____, and _____, on that subject." After years of this it became an inadequate answer for me, so I would force him to give me his answer.

Also in our infrequent talks about theology he made every effort to be charitable. After I had heard of the Van Til-Clark controversy, I brought the subject up to him. It was like pulling eye-teeth to get him to speak on the issues, and what little he did, he tried to keep personalities out of the argument. I really had to find out about this controversy from others, both by reading and talking.

There was a great difference between G.H.C. and me: one that there was no way to resolve, but we both came to accept it to some degree. I am a preacher and teacher, but inside a part of me is a mechanic. I enjoy the ministry, but I also enjoy working with my hands. I have built the buildings of a seminary, which called for logging, sawmilling, truckdriving, plumbing, carpentry, electrical work, etc. G.H.C. was brought up with an understanding that ministry and being a mechanic are two different worlds that should not be mixed. When we visited my wife's parents I usually had a lot of fixing to do around the house, for which he was grateful, but he often made the comment that I would have done better to have spent the time reading some book on theology or philosophy. After I founded a seminary he thought that I should stop the manual work, and act like the president of a seminary—however they act. But eventually I think that we agreed to disagree on this subject: I stopped pushing him to learn which end of a screwdriver was the handle, and he stopped trying to make me someone I wasn't.

From the time that we started Sangre de Cristo Seminary in the mountains of Colorado, Dad Clark taught there in the summers. The first summer was 1978 when he taught "Inspiration of the Scriptures." Thereafter he taught other courses in theology or apologetics. He would often spend several months with us. The summer of 1984 he was with us the entire summer, then returned home to the Chattanooga, Tennessee area long enough to sell his home and pack his belongings and move out here. No matter what course he taught in theology or apologetics, there were two other subjects he also taught along with the course. This is not to say that he did not cover the material in the assigned subject, but he was always insisting that the students think, and think logically. He could not stand "sloppy" thinking. He wanted to know one's Biblical support and/or one's rationale for whatever one said in class or wrote on a paper. The other subject he taught without being asked was outside of the classroom. As most who knew Dr. Clark were aware, he was an avid chess player. He would play with anyone, novice or expert. But he was a serious player, so he taught many students the subject of Humility. He would assist the novice in making moves, but if after being instructed the student insisted on making foolish mistakes, he did not hesitate to win the game.

The death of Dad Clark also helps us to understand the person he was. He came to live with us in September of 1984 and remained in relatively good health for several months for a man of eighty-two. One day in March he complained about his stomach feeling full, and the next day he had to be taken to the local doctor because of some vomiting of blood. He was then admitted to the hospital for about three weeks. The doctor did not want to discharge him, but reluctantly let him return home. He was sorry that he had even gone to the hospital in the first place, and announced that he was dying and the sooner he got it over with the better it would be. He did not want to be readmitted to the hospital or put into a nursing home. Fortunately we were not forced to make this decision against his will. He was bedfast from the time he returned from the hospital and found it difficult, then impossible to retain any fluids or food. Some time before this he had made it clear to all that when he did die he wanted to be buried in the area where he was living. If that was Georgia, bury his remains there; if it was Colorado, have the burial there. When I saw that the end was near, I purchased several lots at a local cemetery here in the valley. I informed him of what I had done, and he indicated that it was all right with him to be buried there. One other item he made clear was that burial expenses were to be kept to a minimum. This request was also adhered to. After returning from the hospital he only lived about one week. During this time he did want someone near him to assist with making him as comfortable as possible, but sought not to be of any more bother than necessary.

As I look back on my relationship with my late

father-in-law, I remember those letters signed "Cordially, G.H.C.," and I wonder what I did with all of them. Probably I threw most of them in the wastebasket. If I could find them in some hidden box, all signed in the same way, I would put those letters in chronological order; then I could read their contents, look at the date, and realize the progression of meaning of each "Cordially, G.H.C." as we came to know and accept each other over the twenty-nine years of our association.

Life With Father, Part 2

Lois A. Zeller

Perhaps the most outstanding thing I remember my father doing with me when I was young was that we frequently took long walks in the evening. We didn't talk a lot, but when I had questions about anything, this is when he taught me. We often talked about the stars on dark nights.

Another means of our education was the vacations we took every summer. He made much advance planning, and we saw most of the outstanding attractions in the United States. Being a college professor, my father had weeks or even months off during the summer (depending on whether he taught in summer school or not). We almost always went somewhere, either to just a church camp or on an extended vacation trip. The first long drive that I remember was made possible because the students at Wheaton decided he needed a car. As he didn't know anything about cars, they went out and bought one. Of course, he paid for this first Ford—the only kind of car he ever had the rest of his life! This was in 1940. The trip was from Wheaton, Illinois to California, as we drove Wheaton students John Lee and his fiancée Miriam out to be married. I was their four-year-old flower girl.

About two years later, our vacation took us to the opposite coast, to a Bible Camp in Maine: Camp Laughing Loon. I remember being so cold in a cabin; and on Stunt Night the group we were in put on the play *Hansel and Gretel,* starring Gordon and Ruth Clark! The crumbs Hansel dropped to show their way through the forest were rocks. Being young, I had the non-speaking part of a tree: a very scared tree who saw her father almost pushed into the stove by a witch.

Subsequent years, our vacations were spent seeing various national parks, Yosemite and Yellowstone being the outstanding ones. In 1954 my father took us to Europe for four months. I even stayed out of college for the spring semester, working at the *Indianapolis Times* newspaper until the first of May when we set sail for France. Before I was born, my parents had lived in France while my father studied at the Sorbonne, and also a short time at the University of Heidelberg, so he wanted his daughter to see where he had been. I enjoyed being able to speak French to people, who seemed to appreciate my efforts. After a month in France, we went to Switzerland, Germany (where people did not respond to my attempts to speak their language), Holland, England, and Scotland. It was a summer which provided us with memories for the rest of our lives.

My father enjoyed music and started me taking piano lessons when I was five years old. I began as a "guinea pig" for Wheaton College students to learn how to teach piano to children, but after about a year of that, I got a regular teacher. While he was teaching at Wheaton, my father always participated in the Christmas presentation of *The Messiah.* Although I never remember his singing solos anywhere, he would sometimes sing when I would play the piano at home. When he was a teenager, he played the cornet. We have a picture of his playing Reveille at Boy Scout camp.

When I started high school, I began to take flute lessons and then played in the high school orchestra. My first two college credits were from taking organ lessons the summer before my regular college schedule began. So his early insistence on practicing music didn't discourage me, but has provided me with a lifelong enjoyment.

Another love my father had was dogs. His boyhood pet was a white bull terrier named Victor, named for the dog on the Victor Talking Machine (Victrola), who belonged to a relative of his uncle who owned the company. My father would make friends with all the dogs he would see on those walks we used to take. When we first moved to Indianapolis in 1945, we would have liked to get a dog, but for six years we couldn't because the lady next door didn't like dogs, and we knew she would not be happy if we fenced our yard in order to get one. So when we moved in 1952, in order to be nearer to Butler University, one of the main considerations was to get a house with a fenced yard. Then we got our dog—a German Shepherd puppy named Solomon Reya, whom we called Rey. How my father loved him. But at the age of 9 months, Rey got distemper—my mother gave him medicine day and night, but to no avail. He died. Then my sister got a mongrel puppy from a dog pound, and named him Herr Oberst, Ober for short. After he also got distemper and died, we found out that a certain germ from a previous owner's dog had infected the house, and a puppy could not live.

Several years later, when I myself was a mother of two sons, we bought a dachshund. When the dog was a year old, my husband Dwight got military orders to Guam, and it was almost impossible to take our dog. So we sent him by train from Albuquerque to Indianapolis, hoping he was old enough to live in my parents' house without succumbing to distemper. So Zephaniah Zeller-Clark lived to the age of 13, and was much beloved by both my parents. We credit him with keeping my father's health good—he had to be walked, even when my father might not have been ambitious enough to take that little bit of exercise without Zephi's need.

My father carefully supervised the education of his two daughters, beginning by teaching me French before I learned English. He even hired a college student to give me French lessons and play French games with me before I started school. Living in Illinois, at the age of 3, I realized I was different—I spoke a different language. So, outside of the home, I did not speak at all, and people evidently assumed I was slow mentally or extremely shy.

My mother then stepped in and taught me to read English, while my father hired a Swiss-reared college student who was fluent in French, to come and play French games with me. When I was six, I was sent to the Christian Grammar School to begin first grade; but when I went home after the first day, and reported to my parents that I had been put into third grade, they didn't believe me at first. Unfortunately, my math ability did not compare with my reading ability, and that gave me trouble all the rest of my school life.

I was in sixth grade when we moved to Indianapolis, and my father sought out the best college preparatory school there was. I was enrolled in a private girls' school (Tudor Hall), where almost everyone was very wealthy and lived in a totally different social class from us. This did not help an already very shy little girl who was two years younger than her classmates. But the social consequences did not matter to a father who wanted the best education for his children. It was in sixth grade that my disability in math surfaced. I had done poorly in fifth grade math, and received ashes in my Christmas stocking as a punishment; but my sixth grade Christmas vacation was even worse. I had to do twenty pages of math every day in order to catch up.

It was a privilege to go to the best college preparatory public high school in Indianapolis. Shortridge High School was strong academically at that time, and my father carefully chose each elective course for me. He allowed me to take one "fun" course, physiography, which was the forerunner of my interest in geology; but he would not let me take biology, or botany, the field in which my mother had a master's degree. Besides required courses, I had to take four years of French and three of German; one semester my father had quite a confrontation with the head of the language department because she had scheduled two classes that I needed for the same class period. He was angry, but the schedule could not be changed, and I had to drop out of French for one semester, because it would be easier to keep up the French on my own, rather than German, the newer language.

My college career was similarly planned: the basic requirements, plus a split French-German major, and a minor in geography. Oh yes, I also took typing, as my father could see some value in that—but of course, nothing practical like Home Ec! He sent me to the Wheaton College Science Station in the Black Hills of South Dakota for a summer course in geology. I liked it so well I wanted to return for another summer; he permitted me to as long as I paid for it myself.

It was fortunate that I enjoyed the languages, but I do remember with dread the many times he would stand over me as I did my homework, trying to make sure every French sentence was grammatically perfect. I disliked grammar, but loved the reading and conversation courses. I suppose my father was pleased when I earned the Alliance Française medal when I graduated from college; but he gave little indication that he noticed. He had one himself, so perhaps he just expected his daughters to do as well.

His great disappointment followed. I was to have gone to France to study after college; but I got married, which dashed his hopes for my future. He had a younger daughter in junior high—and he transferred his vigilance to her education. Fortunately, she delayed her marriage until after the language training, after the European study, and after she taught at Covenant College. By then, she had utilized her mind acceptably, and her marriage did not negate the careful academic background our father had so meticulously planned.

As I write, several years after his death, I see my father's efforts to follow the Biblical principle to "Train up a child in the way he should go, and when he is old he will not depart from it" (Proverbs 22:6). Both in our Christian training and in our schooling he guided his children. If he seemed strict, it was in order to be obedient to God's command to parents. His love for us was not shown outwardly—it was our mother who would praise and encourage us—but my sister and I could tell him with absolute sincerity three days before he died, "You have been a good father to us." He replied, "I have tried to be." He tried, and he succeeded. And we feel the obligation to pass on the heritage of this outstanding servant of God to our children and our children's children.

Logic and Chocolate Ice Cream

Samuel Zinaich, Jr.

When I entered college in 1981, I was like most students in that my exposure to philosophy had been minimal. However, because I was eager to learn, I immersed myself in the philosophical literature required for classes and recommended by teachers. Unfortunately, nearly all my efforts at truth-seeking were inflating my ego. But this was soon to change with my introduction to Dr. Gordon H. Clark.

Although all people are called to the duty to seek the truth, the focus of this call varies from individual to individual. In some cases, this duty is used solely to cross the street without being hit by a car; however, in others, like Dr. Clark, this duty was intensely followed in not only his work, but also his life. Truth, for Dr. Clark, was primary. It was the exposure to both aspects that changed my heart, so to speak.

My initial exposure to Dr. Clark, of course, came through the classroom. I was a little reluctant to take his courses at first, because I was warned that he was not only a tough professor, but he was, at times, a little short with his students. However, after several of his courses, I realized that the warning was not totally accurate. Dr. Clark was, in fact, a tough teacher and, at times, he even seemed a little short with his students; but, as Dr. Clark explained to me, his teaching methods were designed to cause his students to consider the worthiness of the statements that they articulated. Statements, according to Dr. Clark, were worthy of belief only if they were arrived at through a sound deductive process. Therefore, many of our conclusions were reduced to rubble through his careful deductive surgery.

As I have stated before, my initial efforts at philosophical analysis were primarily motivated by an intellectual egotism. However, with the exposure that I gained from Dr. Clark by taking several of his classes, my mind began to change: I began to understand that the search for truth was primary. Although I was pleased with this development in my intellectual interests, there were more unexpected changes that would come with a closer exposure to Dr. Clark's life.

Toward the end of Dr. Clark's teaching career at Covenant College, several students, including myself, petitioned Dr. Clark to teach a private course on logic, because we were dissatisfied with the required logic course that was presently being taught. Dr. Clark was pleased with this request and agreed to instruct us. Coincidentally, Dr. Clark had just finished a manuscript of a book that would later be published, entitled *Logic*.

The course was taught primarily at my apartment, and we met three times a week in the evening. Before class, everybody, including Dr. Clark, met for dinner. Normally, Dr. Clark would give the dinner blessing, because every time I prayed, Dr. Clark would comment on my bad grammar and that made me too nervous. After the prayer and during dinner, we would be treated to discussions on all sorts of topics. For example, Dr. Clark would talk about the Scriptures, history, poetry, art, politics, language, and chess moves, just to name a few. He also talked about his daughters and his late wife, where he had studied, and the logical problems with Cornelius Van Til's work. A big highlight of the evenings would be the songs he would sing for my children in French and Greek.

After dinner, with large bowls of chocolate ice cream in our laps (Dr. Clark loved chocolate ice cream), the class would begin. Inevitably questions would spring from the text and the discussion would slowly slip from the methods of necessary inference to the more theoretical side of the philosophy of logic. Dr. Clark seemed to thrive on the discussion and was always ready to answer one more question. After class, it was usually late, and Dr. Clark would politely thank our wives for dinner and then leave. It was during this time at my apartment and through all the conversations that it became clear to me that Dr. Clark's desire for the truth extended to all the areas of his life, not just to his academic pursuits. Dr. Clark was never satisfied with the uncritical, popular opinions about any topic that he thought and talked about. Instead, he was concerned with the first principles of any subject he considered: those primary ideas that all subjects begin with. It wasn't long after this realization that I began to follow Dr. Clark's example.

It is my privilege to offer this brief description of a man who was my model and mentor. I know there is nothing novel about my recollections of Clark, because I know others that were influenced by Dr. Clark in the same way. Philosophy, for Dr. Clark, was an act of worship, and this is what he taught all his students.

Index

The Works of Gordon H. Clark[1]

Books

Atonement, The. Jefferson, Maryland: The Trinity Foundation, 1987.

Behaviorism and Christianity. Jefferson, Maryland: The Trinity Foundation, 1982.

Biblical Doctrine of Man, The. Jefferson, Maryland: The Trinity Foundation, 1984.

Biblical Predestination. Nutley, New Jersey: The Presbyterian and Reformed Publishing Company, 1969. Reprinted in *Predestination,* 1987.

Christian Philosophy of Education, A. Jefferson, Maryland: The Trinity Foundation, 1988 [1946].

Christian View of Men and Things, A. Grand Rapids, Michigan: The Wm. B. Eerdmans Publishing Company, 1952.

Clark Speaks From The Grave. Jefferson, Maryland: The Trinity Foundation, 1986.

Colossians. Jefferson, Maryland: The Trinity Foundation, 1989 [1979].

[1]This bibliography is incomplete. It is the most extensive Clark bibliography ever published, but more Clark essays and reviews come to light each month, in addition to new Clark essays and books being published by The Trinity Foundation. If any reader is aware of any Clark writings not listed here, please send a copy or at least a citation to the editor at The Trinity Foundation. Thank you.

Concept of Biblical Authority, The. Nutley, New Jersey: The Presbyterian and Reformed Publishing Company, 1979. Reprinted in *God's Hammer: The Bible and Its Critics,* 1987 [1982].

Dewey. Philadelphia, Pennsylvania: The Presbyterian and Reformed Publishing Company, 1960.

Empedocles and Anaxagoras in Aristotle's De Anima. (Doctoral Thesis, University of Pennsylvania), Philadelphia, Pennsylvania, March 1929. (Unpublished.)

Ephesians. Jefferson, Maryland: The Trinity Foundation, 1985.

Faith and Saving Faith. Jefferson, Maryland: The Trinity Foundation, 1983.

First Corinthians: A Contemporary Commentary. Nutley, New Jersey: The Presbyterian and Reformed Publishing Company, 1975.

First John. Jefferson, Maryland: The Trinity Foundation, 1980.

God's Hammer: The Bible and Its Critics. Jefferson, Maryland: The Trinity Foundation, 1987 [1982].

Historiography: Secular and Religious. Nutley, New Jersey: The Craig Press, 1971.

History of Philosophy, A. Seymour G. Martin, Gordon H. Clark, Francis P. Clarke, and Chester T. Ruddick. New York: F.S. Crofts and Company, 1941.

Incarnation, The. Jefferson, Maryland: The Trinity Foundation, 1988.

In Defense of Theology. Milford, Michigan: Mott Media, 1984.

Johannine Logos, The. Jefferson, Maryland: The Trinity Foundation, 1989 [1972].

Karl Barth's Theological Method. Philadelphia, Pennsylvania: The Presbyterian and Reformed Publishing Company, 1963.

Language and Theology. Jefferson, Maryland: The Trinity Foundation, 1980.

Logic. Jefferson, Maryland: The Trinity Foundation, 1988 [1985].

Logical Criticisms of Textual Criticism. Jefferson, Maryland: The Trinity Foundation, 1986.

Pastoral Epistles, The. Jefferson, Maryland: The Trinity Foundation, 1984.

Peter Speaks Today: A Devotional Commentary on First Peter. Philadelphia, Pennsylvania: The Presbyterian and Reformed Publishing Company, 1969. Reprinted in *I and II Peter,* 1980.

I and II Peter. Phillipsburg, New Jersey: Presbyterian and Reformed Publishing Company, 1980.

II Peter, A Short Commentary. Nutley, New Jersey: Presbyterian and Reformed Publishing Company, 1972. Reprinted in *I and II Peter,* 1980.

Philosophy of Gordon H. Clark, The. Ronald H. Nash, editor. Philadelphia, Pennsylvania: The Presbyterian and Reformed Publishing Company, 1968.

Philosophy of Science and Belief in God, The. Jefferson, Maryland: The Trinity Foundation, 1987 [1964].

Predestination. Phillipsburg, New Jersey: Presbyterian and Reformed Publishing Company, 1987.

Predestination in the Old Testament. Nutley, New Jersey: The Presbyterian and Reformed Publishing Company, 1978. Reprinted in *Predestination,* 1987.

Readings in Ethics. Gordon H. Clark and T.V. Smith, editors. New York: F.S. Crofts and Company, first edition, 1931.

Readings in Ethics. Gordon H. Clark and T.V. Smith, editors. New York: F.S. Crofts and Company, second edition, 1935. (Chapter on Spinoza added.)

Religion, Reason and Revelation. Jefferson, Maryland: The Trinity Foundation, 1986 [1961]

Selections from Early Greek Philosophy, M.C. Nahm. (Translations of Democritean material). New York: F.S. Crofts and Company, 1934.

Selections from Hellenistic Philosophy. New York: Appleton-Century-Crofts, 1940.

Thales to Dewey: A History of Philosophy. Jefferson, Maryland: The Trinity Foundation, 1989 [1957].

I and II Thessalonians. Jefferson, Maryland: The Trinity Foundation, 1986.

Three Types of Religious Philosophy. Jefferson, Maryland: The Trinity Foundation, 1989 [1973].

Trinity, The. Jefferson, Maryland: The Trinity Foundation, 1985.
What Do Presbyterians Believe? Phillipsburg, New Jersey: The Presbyterian and Reformed Publishing Company, 1985 [1965].
What Presbyterians Believe. Philadelphia, Pennsylvania: The Presbyterian and Reformed Publishing Company, 1956.
William James. Philadelphia, Pennsylvania: The Presbyterian and Reformed Publishing Company, 1963.

Articles

Abelard. *Encyclopedia of Christianity* (National Foundation for Christian Education), 1964.
Activism. *Baker's Dictionary of Christian Ethics* (Carl F.H. Henry, editor), Washington, D.C.: Canon Press, 1973.
Adoption. *The Southern Presbyterian Journal,* January 5, 1955.
Agnosticism. *Encyclopedia of Christianity* (National Foundation for Christian Education), 1964.
Alexandrian School. *Collier's Encyclopedia.* New York: P.F. Collier and Son, 1949.
Altruism. *Baker's Dictionary of Christian Ethics* (Carl F.H. Henry, editor), Washington, D.C.: Canon Press, 1973.
Anarchism. *Baker's Dictionary of Christian Ethics* (Carl F.H. Henry, editor), Washington, D.C.: Canon Press, 1973.
Anselm. *Encyclopedia of Christianity* (National Foundation for Christian Education), 1964.
Antithesis. *Baker's Dictionary of Christian Ethics* (Carl F.H. Henry, editor), Washington, D.C.: Canon Press, 1973.
Apologetics. *Encyclopedia of Christianity* (National Foundation for Christian Education), 1964.
Apologetics. *Contemporary Evangelical Thought* (Carl F.H. Henry, editor), Grand Rapids, Michigan: Baker Book House, 1957.
Appeal to Fundamentalists. An. *The Presbyterian Guardian,* March 10, 1943.

Aquinas, *Baker's Dictionary of Christian Ethics* (Carl F.H. Henry, editor), Washington, D.C.: Canon Press, 1973.

Art and the Gospel. *The Trinity Review,* Number 24. March/April, 1982.

Assault Upon the Living God (Contributor). *Christianity Today,* March 15, 1968.

Assurance. *The Southern Presbyterian Journal,* January 19, 1955.

Atheism. *Baker's Dictionary of Christian Ethics* (Carl F.H. Henry, editor), Washington, D.C.: Canon Press, 1973.

Atheism. *The Trinity Review,* Number 32. July/August 1983.

Augustine. *Baker's Dictionary of Christian Ethics* (Carl F.H. Henry, editor), Washington, D.C.: Canon Press, 1973.

Augustine of Hippo. *Encyclopedia of Christianity* (National Foundation for Christian Education), 1964.

Baptism. *The Southern Presbyterian Journal,* March 16, 1955.

Barth's Critique of Modernism. *Christianity Today,* January 5, 1962.

Barth's Turnabout from the Biblical Norm (excerpt from *Karl Barth's Theological Method*). *Christianity Today,* January 4, 1963.

Beginnings of Greek Philosophy, The. *A History of Philosophical Systems* (Vergilius Ferm, editor), New York: The Philosophical Library, 1950.

Behaviorism. *Baker's Dictionary of Christian Ethics* (Carl F.H. Henry, editor), Washington, D.C.: Canon Press, 1973.

Bible As Truth, The. *Bibliotheca Sacra,* April 1957. Reprinted in *God's Hammer: The Bible and its Critics,* 1987 [1982].

Bonaventura. *Encyclopedia of Christianity* (National Foundation for Christian Education), 1968.

Bultmann's Historiography. *Jesus of Nazareth: Saviour and Lord* (Carl F.H. Henry, editor), Grand Rapids, Michigan: Eerdmans, 1966.

Bultmann's Three-Storied Universe. *Christianity Today,* March 2, 1962.

Calvinistic Ethics. *Baker's Dictionary of Christian Ethics* (Carl F.H. Henry, editor), Washington, D.C.: Canon Press, 1973.

Can Moral Education Be Grounded in Naturalism? (Paper presented to the fourth annual meeting of the Evangelical Theological Society, Wheaton, Illinois, 1952), *Bulletin of the Evangelical Theological Society,* Fall 1958.

Capital Punishment. *Baker's Dictionary of Christian Ethics* (Carl F.H. Henry, editor), Washington, D.C.: Canon Press, 1973.

Capital Punishment and the Bible. *Christianity Today,* February 1, 1960.

Carneades. *Collier's Encyclopedia,* New York: P.F. Collier and Son, 1949.

Censures and Councils. *The Southern Presbyterian Journal,* April 13, 1955.

Christ the Mediator. *The Southern Presbyterian Journal,* December 1, 1954.

Christendom's Key Issue: 25 Scholars' Views. *Christianity Today,* October 12, 1959.

Christian Aesthetics. *The Trinity Review,* Number 67. May/June 1989.

Christian and the Law, The. *HIS,* October 1957. Reprinted in *The Trinity Review,* Number 1. March 1979.

Christian Liberty. *The Southern Presbyterian Journal,* February 16, 1955.

Christian Philosophy of Education, A. *The Trinity Review,* Number 61. May/June 1988.

Church, The. *The Southern Presbyterian Journal,* March 23, 1955.

Civil Magistrate, The. *The Southern Presbyterian Journal,* March 30, 1955.

Clark Speaks from the Grave. *The Trinity Review,* Number 46. November/December 1985.

Classical Apologetics. *The Trinity Review,* Number 45. September/October 1985.

Cleanthes. *Collier's Encyclopedia,* New York: P.F. Collier and Son, 1976.

Comments on Mr. Verduin's Essay. *Christianity Today,* May 21, 1965.

Concerning Free Will. *Reformed Presbyterian Advocate,* August-September, 1961.

Concerning Justification. *Christianity Today,* March 16, 1973.

Cosmic Time: A Critique of the Concept in Herman Dooyeweerd. *The Gordon Review,* September 1956.

Cosmological Argument, The. *The Trinity Review,* Number 7, September 1979.

Covenant, The. *The Southern Presbyterian Journal,* November 24, 1954.

Creation. *The Southern Presbyterian Journal,* November 10, 1954.

Creeds. *The Southern Presbyterian Journal,* October 6, 1954.

Cynicism. *Baker's Dictionary of Christian Ethics* (Carl F.H. Henry, editor), Washington, D.C.: Canon Press, 1973.

Democritus. *American People's Encyclopedia,* Chicago: The Spencer Press, 1948.

Destiny. *Zondervan Pictorial Encyclopedia of the Bible* (Merrill C. Tenney, editor), Grand Rapids, Michigan: Zondervan Publishing House, 1975.

Determinism. *Baker's Dictionary of Christian Ethics* (Carl F. H. Henry, editor), Washington, D.C.: Canon Press, 1973.

Determinism and Responsibility. *The Evangelical Quarterly* (London), January 1932.

Diogenes. *Collier's Encyclopedia,* New York: P.F. Collier and Son, 1950.

Dispensationalism. *The Trinity Review,* Number 12. March/ April 1980.

Divine Attributes, The. *Baker's Dictionary of Theology* (Everett F. Harrison, editor), Grand Rapids, Michigan: Baker Book House, 1960.

Eclecticism. *Collier's Encyclopedia,* New York: P.F. Collier and Son, 1949.

Effectual Calling. *The Southern Presbyterian Journal,* December 29, 1954.

Egoism. *Baker's Dictionary of Christian Ethics* (Carl F.H. Henry, editor), Washington, D.C.: Canon Press, 1973.

Emanation. *American People's Encyclopedia,* Chicago: The Spencer Press, 1948.

Empiricism. *Encyclopedia of Christianity* (National Foundation for Christian Education), 1968.

Enlightenment, The. *Encyclopedia of Christianity* (National Foundation for Christian Education), 1968.

Epictetus. *Collier's Encyclopedia,* New York: P.F. Collier and Son, 1949.

Epicureanism. *Encyclopedia of Christianity* (National Foundation for Christian Education), 1968.

Epicureans. *Zondervan Pictorial Encyclopedia of the Bible* (Merrill C. Tenney, editor), Grand Rapids, Michigan: Zondervan Publishing House, 1975.

Epistemology. *Encyclopedia of Christianity* (National Foundation for Christian Education), 1968.

Eriugena, John Scotus. *Encyclopedia of Christianity* (National Foundation for Christian Education), 1968.

Eternity. *Zondervan Pictorial Encyclopedia of the Bible* (Merrill C. Tenney, editor), Grand Rapids, Michigan: Zondervan Publishing House, 1975.

Ethics. *Zondervan Pictorial Encyclopedia of the Bible* (Merrill C. Tenney, editor), Grand Rapids, Michigan: Zondervan Publishing House, 1975

Ethics, History of. *Baker's Dictionary of Christian Ethics* (Carl F.H. Henry, editor), Washington, D.C.: Canon Press, 1973.

Ethics of Abortion, The. *The Trinity Review,* Number 25. May/June 1982.

Evangelicalism. *Encyclopedia of Christianity* (National Foundation for Christian Education), 1968

Evangelical Theological Society Tomorrow, The. *Bulletin of the Evangelical Theological Society,* Winter 1966. Reprinted in *God's Hammer: The Bible and Its Critics,* 1987 [1982].

Existence of God, The. *Encyclopedia of Christianity* (National Foundation for Christian Education), 1968.

Faith. *Baker's Dictionary of Christian Ethics* (Carl F.H. Henry, editor), Washington, D.C.: Canon Press, 1973.

Faith and Reason. *Christianity Today,* February 18 and March 4, 1957.

Faith Without a Focus Is Also Dead. *Christianity Today,* December 5, 1968.

Fate. *Baker's Dictionary of Christian Ethics* (Carl F.H. Henry, editor), Washington, D.C.: Canon Press, 1973.

Feuerbach, Ludwig A. *Encyclopedia of Christianity* (National Foundation for Christian Education), 1968.

Foreknowledge. *Encyclopedia of Christianity* (National Foundation for Christian Education), 1968.

Foreordination. *Encyclopedia of Christianity* (National Foundation for Christian Education), 1968.

Free Will. *The Southern Presbyterian Journal,* December 22, 1954.

Fresh Look At the Hypothesis of Evolution, A. *Christianity Today,* September 1, 1958.

Fruits of the Reformation in Philosophy and Ethics . . . 'A Complete Reversal of Scholasticism'. *Christianity Today,* October 22, 1965.

Gnosticism. *Encyclopedia of Christianity* (National Foundation for Christian Education), 1968.

God. *Baker's Dictionary of Theology* (Everett F. Harrison, editor), Grand Rapids, Michigan: Baker Book House, 1960.

God and Logic. *The Trinity Review,* Number 16. November/December 1980.

God's Countdown: 1960 (Contributor). *Christianity Today,* December 21, 1959.

Good Works. *The Southern Presbyterian Journal,* February 9, 1955.

Greek Ethics. *Baker's Dictionary of Christian Ethics* (Carl F.H. Henry, editor), Washington, D.C.: Canon Press, 1973.

Greek Religion and Philosophy. *Zondervan Pictorial Encyclopedia of the Bible* (Merrill C. Tenney, editor), Grand Rapids, Michigan: Zondervan Publishing House, 1975.

Guest Editorial. *Journal of the Evangelical Theological Society,* Spring 1969.

Hamilton's Theory of Language and Inspiration. *Journal of the Evangelical Theological Society,* 1972. Reprinted in *God's Ham-*

mer: The Bible and Its Critics, 1987 [1982].

Happiness. *Baker's Dictionary of Christian Ethics* (Carl F.H. Henry, editor), Washington, D.C.: Canon Press, 1973.

Hard Saying, A. *The Southern Presbyterian Journal,* October 27, 1954.

Healthy, Sick, or Dead? *The Southern Presbyterian Journal,* November 17, 1954.

Hedonism. *Baker's Dictionary of Christian Ethics* (Carl F.H. Henry, editor), Washington, D.C.: Canon Press, 1973.

Hellenistic and Roman Schools of Philosophy. *A History of Philosophical Systems* (Vergilius Ferm, editor), New York: the Philosophical Library, 1950.

Heritage of Irrationalism, A (excerpt from *Karl Barth's Theological Method). Christianity Today,* October 9, 1964.

Holy Scripture. *Bulletin of the Evangelical Theological Society,* Winter 1963. Reprinted in *God's Hammer: The Bible and Its Critics,* 1987 [1982].

How Do We Learn? *The Trinity Review,* Number 34. November/December 1983.

How Does Man Know God? *The Trinity Review,* Number 68. July/August 1989.

How May I Know the Bible Is Inspired? *(Can I Trust the Bible?* Howard Vos, editor). Chicago: Moody Press, 1963. Reprinted in *God's Hammer: The Bible and Its Critics,* 1987 [1982].

Humanism. *Baker's Dictionary of Christian Ethics* (Carl F.H. Henry, editor), Washington, D.C.: Canon Press, 1973.

Idealistic Ethics. *Baker's Dictionary of Christian Ethics* (Carl F.H. Henry, editor), Washington, D.C.: Canon Press, 1973.

Image and Likeness of God, The. *The Trinity Review,* Number 33. September/October 1983.

Image of God. *Baker's Dictionary of Christian Ethics* (Carl F.H. Henry, editor), Washington, D.C.: Canon Press, 1973.

Image of God in Man, The. *Journal of the Evangelical Theological Society,* Fall 1969.

Immutability. *Wycliffe Bible Encyclopedia.* (Howard Vos, Charles Pfeiffer, John Rea, editors) Chicago: Moody Press, 1975.

In the Beginning. *The Trinity Review,* Number 40. November/ December 1984.

Incarnation: Fact or Theory? *Christianity Today,* December 10, 1956.

Intuition. *Baker's Dictionary of Christian Ethics* (Carl F.H. Henry, editor), Washington, D.C.: Canon Press, 1973.

Irrationalism. *Baker's Dictionary of Christian Ethics* (Carl F.H. Henry, editor), Washington, D.C.: Canon Press, 1973.

Is Christianity Unique? *Christianity Today,* December 21, 1959.

James, William. *Baker's Dictionary of Christian Ethics* (Carl F.H. Henry, editor), Washington, D.C.: Canon Press, 1973.

John Dewey. *Baker's Dictionary of Christian Ethics* (Carl F.H. Henry, editor), Washington, D.C.: Canon Press, 1973.

Justification. *The Southern Presbyterian Journal,* December 8, 1954.

Kant. *Baker's Dictionary of Christian Ethics* (Carl F.H. Henry, editor), Washington, D.C.: Canon Press, 1973.

Know, Knowledge. *Zondervan Pictorial Encyclopedia of the Bible* (Merrill C. Tenney, editor), Grand Rapids, Michigan: Zondervan Publishing Company, 1975.

Knowledge. *Baker's Dictionary of Theology* (Everett F. Harrison, editor), Grand Rapids, Michigan: Baker Book House, 1960.

Knowledge and Ignorance. *The Southern Presbyterian Journal,* October 13, 1954.

Language and Logic. *The Gordon Review,* January 12, 1955.

Legalism. *Baker's Dictionary of Christian Ethics* (Carl F.H. Henry, editor), Washington, D.C.: Canon Press, 1973.

Liberalism. *Wycliffe Bible Encyclopedia* (Howard Vos, Charles Pfeiffer, John Rea, editors), Chicago: Moody Press, 1975.

Logic and Language. *The Gordon Review,* February 1956.

Logical Criticisms of Textual Criticism. *The Trinity Review,* Number 36. March/April 1984.

Lord God of Truth. *Ambitious To Be Well-Pleasing* (Allen Guelzo, editor). Jefferson, Maryland: The Trinity Foundation, 1986.

Lord's Supper, The. *The Southern Presbyterian Journal,* April 6, 1955.

Mindless Men: Behaviorism and Christianity. *The Trinity Review,* Number 14. July/August 1980.

Miracles. *Zondervan Pictorial Encyclopedia of the Bible,* (Merrill C. Tenney, editor), Grand Rapids, Michigan: Zondervan Publishing Company, 1975.

Miracles, History, and Natural Law. *The Evangelical Quarterly* (London), January 1940.

Modern Christianity's Crucial Junctures. *Christianity Today,* October 11, 1963.

Modern Science and Belief in God (excerpt from *The Philosophy of Science and Belief in God). Christianity Today,* August 27, 1965.

Moon Shot: Its Meaning to 25 Scholars (Contributor).*Christianity Today,* October 13, 1958.

More Questions on Barth's Views (Contributor). *Christianity Today,* January 5, 1962.

Natural Law and Revelation (Anonymous guest editorial). *Christianity Today,* June 24, 1957.

Naturalism. *The Southern Presbyterian Journal,* March 7, 1962.

Nature of the Physical Universe, The. *Christian Faith and Modern Theology* (Carl F.H. Henry, editor), New York: Channel Press, 1963.

Neoorthodoxy. *Wycliffe Bible Encyclopedia* (Howard Vos, Charles Pfeiffer, John Rea, editors), Chicago: Moody Press, 1975.

New Discovery in the Quest of the Historical Jesus, A. *Christianity Today,* January 15, 1971. Reprinted in *The Trinity Review,* Number 60. March/April 1988.

Next Ten Years, The (Contributor). *Christianity Today,* October 9, 1964.

Number of the Beast, The. *The Trinity Review,* Number 38. July/August 1984.

Oaths. *Baker's Dictionary of Christian Ethics* (Carl F.H. Henry, editor), Washington, D.C.: Canon Press, 1973.

On the Primacy of the Intellect. *Westminster Theological Journal,* May 1943.

Ordination of Women, The. *The Trinity Review,* Number 17. January/February 1981. Reprinted in *The Pastoral Epistles,*

Jefferson, Maryland: The Trinity Foundation, 1984; and in *Scripture Twisting in the Seminaries, Part 1: Feminism,* John W. Robbins, 1985.

Perseverance. *The Southern Presbyterian Journal,* February 23, 1955.

Philo Judeus. *Zondervan Pictorial Encyclopedia of the Bible,* (Merrill C. Tenney, editor), Grand Rapids, Michigan: Zondervan Publishing Company, 1975.

Philosophy. *Zondervan Pictorial Encyclopedia of the Bible* (Merrill C. Tenney, editor), Grand Rapids, Michigan: Zondervan Publishing Company, 1975.

Philosophy in the Sixties. *Christianity Today,* May 9, 1960.

Plotinus. *Collier's Encyclopedia,* New York: P.F. Collier and Son, 1949.

Plotinus on the Eternity of the World. *The Philosophical Review,* March 1949.

Plotinus' Theory of Empirical Responsibility. *The New Scholasticism,* January 1943.

Plotinus' Theory of Sensation. *The Philosophical Review,* July 1942.

Pragmatism. *Baker's Dictionary of Christian Ethics.* (Carl F.H. Henry, editor), Washington, D.C.: Canon Press, 1973.

Problem of Motion, The. *The Gordon Review,* Winter 1958.

Protestant World View, A. *The Trinity Review,* Numbers 2 and 3. April and May, 1979.

Protestant-Roman Unity: 25 Scholars' Views (Contributor). *Christianity Today,* October 10, 1960.

Providence. *The Southern Presbyterian Journal,* November 3, 1954.

Puritans and Situation Ethics, The. *The Trinity Review,* Number 65. January/February 1989.

Questions on Barth's Theology (Contributor). *Christianity Today,* July 3, 1961.

Reference to Plotinus in Liddell and Scott, A. *The American Journal of Philology,* July 1944.

Relationship of Public Education to Christianity, The. *The Trinity Review,* Number 43. May/June 1985.

Repentance. *The Southern Presbyterian Journal,* February 2, 1955.

Responsibility. *Baker's Dictionary of Christian Ethics* (Carl F.H. Henry, editor), Washington D.C.: Canon Press, 1973.

Resurrection, The. *Christianity Today,* April 15, 1957.

Resurrection and Judgment. *The Southern Presbyterian Journal,* April 20, 1955.

Revealed Religion. *Christianity Today,* December 17, 1965. Reprinted in *God's Hammer: The Bible and Its Critics,* 1987 [1982].

Romans. *The Biblical Expositor* (Carl F.H. Henry, editor), Philadelphia, Pennsylvania: A.J. Holman Company, 1960.

Sacraments, The. *The Southern Presbyterian Journal,* March 9, 1955.

Sanctification. *The Southern Presbyterian Journal,* December 15, 1954.

Saving Faith. *The Southern Presbyterian Journal,* January 26, 1955.

Saving Faith. *The Trinity Review,* Number 10, December 1979.

Scholars' Panel Identifies Contemporary Idols (Contributor). *Christianity Today,* October 13, 1961.

Science and Truth. *The Trinity Review,* Number 19. May/June 1981.

Sighting the Final Third of the Twentieth Century ... The Church and the Nation (Contributor). *Christianity Today,* January 20, 1967.

Situational Ethics. *Baker's Dictionary of Christian Ethics* (Carl F.H. Henry, editor), Washington, D.C.: Canon Press, 1973.

Skepticism. *Baker's Dictionary of Christian Ethics* (Carl F.H. Henry, editor), Washington, D.C.: Canon Press, 1973.

Sovereignty of God, The. *The Trinity Review,* Number 28. November/December 1982.

Special Divine Revelation as Rational. *Revelation and the Bible* (Carl F. H. Henry, editor), Grand Rapids, Michigan: Baker Book House, 1959. Reprinted in *God's Hammer: The Bible and Its Critics,* 1987 [1982].

Spontaneity and Monstrosity in Aristotle. *The New Scholasticism,* January 1934.

Stoicism. *Collier's Encyclopedia,* New York: P.F. Collier and Son, 1949.

Stoics. *Zondervan Pictorial Encyclopedia of the Bible* (Merrill C. Tenney, editor), Grand Rapids, Michigan: Zondervan Publishing House, 1975.

Textual Criticism. *The Trinity Review,* Number 37. May/June 1984.

Theism. *Zondervan Pictorial Encyclopedia of the Bible* (Merrill C. Tenney, editor), Grand Rapids, Michigan: Zondervan Publishing Company, 1975.

Theory of Time in Plotinus, The. *The Philosophical Review,* July 1944.

Thomas Aquinas. *Encyclopedia of Christianity* (National Foundation for Christian Education), 1964.

Timaeus or Plato? *The New Scholasticism,* October 1934.

Time and Eternity. *The Trinity Review,* Number 21. September/October 1981. Reprinted in *God's Hammer: The Bible and Its Critics,* 1982.

I and II Timothy. *The Trinity Review,* Number 30. March/April 1983.

Toronto School, The. *The Trinity Review,* Number 6. August 1979.

Traducianism. *The Trinity Review,* Number 26. July/August 1982.

Trinity. *Wycliffe Bible Encyclopedia* (Howard Vos, Charles Pfeiffer, John Rea, editors), Chicago: Moody Press, 1975.

Trinity, The. *The Southern Presbyterian Journal,* October 20, 1954.

Trinity, The. *The Trinity Review,* Number 9. November 1979.

Trouble with Humanism, The. *Christianity Today,* May 12, 1967.

Truth. *Baker's Dictionary of Theology* (Everett F. Harrison, editor), Grand Rapids, Michigan: Baker Book House, 1960.

Two Religions. *Christianity Today,* April 9, 1965.

Two Translations of Plotinus. *The New Scholasticism,* January 1938.

Utilitarianism. *Baker's Dictionary of Christian Ethics* (Carl F.H. Henry, editor), Washington, D.C.: Canon Press, 1973.

Values. *Baker's Dictionary of Christian Ethics* (Carl F.H. Henry, editor), Washington, D.C.: Canon Press, 1973.

Variety of Versions, The. *The Trinity Review,* Number 35, January/February 1984.

Verbal Inspiration: Yesterday and Today. *The Southern Presbyterian Journal,* September 12, 1956. Reprinted in *God's Hammer: The Bible and Its Critics,* 1987 [1982].

What Is Truth? *Presbuterion,* Fall 1980. Reprinted in *God's Hammer: The Bible and Its Critics,* 1987.

Wisdom in First Corinthians. *Journal of the Evangelical Theological Society,* Fall 1972.

Word of God, The. *The Southern Presbyterian Journal,* September 29, 1954.

Worship and Vows. *The Southern Presbyterian Journal,* March 2, 1955.

Zeno. *Collier's Encyclopedia.* New York: P.F. Collier and Son, 1949.

Book Reviews

Act and Being. Dietrich Bonhoeffer. *Christianity Today,* June 22, 1962.

Albert Schweitzer. Jacques Feschotte. *Christianity Today,* September 1, 1958.

Anselm: Fides Quaerens Intellectum. Karl Barth. *Christianity Today,* June 5, 1961.

Aristotle's Theory of the Infinite. Abraham Edel. *The New Scholasticism,* January 1935.

Challenge of Our Age, The. Hendrik Hart. *Blue Banner Faith and Life,* October-December 1974.

Christ and Christian. Nels F. S. Ferré. *Christianity Today,* January 5, 1959.

Christian Commitment: An Apologetic. Edward John Carnell. *Christianity Today,* September 2, 1957.

Christianity and World Issues. T. B. Maston. *Christianity Today,* October 14, 1957.

Classical Apologetics. R.C. Sproul, John Gerstner, and Arthur Lindsley, *The Trinity Review,* Number 45. September/October 1985.

Coming World Civilization, The. William Ernest Hocking. *Christianity Today,* May 26, 1958.

Conflict With Rome. G.C. Berkouwer. *Christianity Today,* February 17, 1958.

Conscience and Its Rights to Freedom. Eric D'Arcy. *Christianity Today,* April 27, 1962.

Defence of Theological Ethics, A. G.F. Woods. *Christianity Today,* September 16, 1966.

Deliverance to the Captives. Karl Barth. *Christianity Today,* June 5, 1961.

Divine Perfection: Possible Ideas of God. Frederick Sontag. *Christianity Today,* April 13, 1962.

Enforcement of Morals, The. Patrick Devlin. *Christianity Today,* October 8, 1965.

Essays in Applied Christianity. Reinhold Niebuhr. *Christianity Today,* January 4, 1960.

Essence of Plotinus, The. Grace H. Turnball. *The New Scholasticism,* January 1935.

Ethics and Science. Henry Morgenau. *Christianity Today,* December 18, 1964.

Experience and God. John E. Smith. *Christianity Today,* November 8, 1968.

Fabric of Paul Tillich's Theology, The. David H. Kelsey. *Christianity Today,* June 23, 1967.

History of Religions, Essays in Methodology, The. Edited by Eliade and Kitagawa. *Christianity Today,* February 15, 1960.

Humanity of God, The. Karl Barth. *Christianity Today,* April 25, 1960.

Idea of Transcendence in the Philosophy of Karl Jaspers, The. R.D. Knudsen. *The Gordon Review,* Summer 1959.

In the Beginning, God. William M. Logan. *The Gordon Review,* Winter 1958.

In the Twilight of Western Thought. Herman Dooyeweerd. *Christianity Today,* August 29, 1960.

Issues in Science and Religion. Ian G. Barbout. *Christianity Today,* October 28, 1966.

Karl Barth on God. Sebastian A. Matczak. *Christianity Today,* March 1, 1963.

Karl Barth's Doctrine of Holy Scripture. Klaas Runia. *Christianity Today,* July 6, 1962.

Late Medieval Mysticism. Edited by Ray C. Petry. *Christianity Today,* May 12, 1958.

Limits of Reason, The. George Boas. *Christianity Today,* May 8, 1961.

Many-Faced Argument, The. Edited by John Hick and Arthur C. Magill. *Christianity Today,* January 5, 1968.

Myth and Truth. John Knox. *Bulletin of the Evangelical Theological Society,* Summer 1967.

Persons in Relation. John Macmurray. *Christianity Today,* December 22, 1961.

Perspectives in 19th and 20th Century Protestant Theology. Paul Tillich. *Christianity Today,* June 23, 1967.

Philosophical Study of Religion, A. David Hugh Freeman. *Christianity Today,* October 23, 1964.

Philosophy of St. Bonaventure, The. Etienne Gilson. *Westminster Theological Journal,* November 1938.

Platonic Legend, The. Warner Fite. *The New Scholasticism,* January 1935.

Principles of Christian Ethics, The. Albert C. Knudson. *Westminster Theological Journal.*

Relativism, Knowledge and Faith. Gordon D. Kaufman. *Christianity Today,* June 20, 1960.

Revolt Against Heaven. Kenneth Hamilton. *The Gordon Review,* Spring 1966.

Sacra Doctrina: Reason and Revelation in Aquinas. Per Eric Persson. *Christianity Today,* October 9, 1970.

Scepticism and Historical Knowledge. Jack W. Meiland. *The Gordon Review,* Spring 1966.

Scholastic Miscellany: Anselm to Ockham, A. Edited by Eugene R. Fairweather. *Christianity Today,* January 21, 1957.

School of Faith, The. Thomas F. Torrance. *Christianity Today,* July 4, 1960.

Sense and Nonsense in Religion. Sten H. Stenson. *Christianity Today,* July 4, 1969.

Social Ethics of Reinhold Niebuhr, The. Theodore Minnema. *Christianity Today,* January 4, 1960.

Social Responsibilities of Organized Labor. John A. Fitch. *Christianity Today,* June 22, 1959.

Speculation in Pre-Christian Philosophy. Richard Kroner. *Christianity Today,* March 18, 1957.

Tennant's Philosophical Theology. Delton Lewis Scudder. *Westminster Theological Journal.*

Theological Ethics. James Sellers. *Christianity Today,* July 22, 1966.

Theories of Revelation. H.C. McDonald. *Christianity Today,* September 13, 1963.

To Prod the Slumbering Giant (Association for the Advancement of Christian Scholarship). ("Toronto Scholarship"), *Blue Banner Faith and Life,* July-September, 1975.

Understanding the Scripture. A.H. DeGraaff and C.G. Seerveld. ("How to Let the Bible Confuse You"), *Episcopal Recorder,* February 1972.

Varieties of Christian Apologetics. Bernard Ramm. *Christianity Today,* July 20, 1962.

Vision of Paul Tillich, The. Carl J. Armbruster. *Christianity Today,* June 23, 1967.

What About Speaking in Tongues? Anthony A. Hoekema. *The Gordon Review,* Winter 1967.

Words and Images. E.L. Mascall. *Christianity Today,* August 18, 1958.

Words and the WORD. Kenneth Hamilton, ("Hamilton's Theory of Language and Inspiration"), *Journal of the Evangelical Theological Society,* Winter 1972.

Letters

(Agape). *Christianity Today,* March 2, 1959.
(Biblical separation). *Christianity Today,* December 9, 1957.

(Biblical separation). *Christianity Today,* May 26, 1958.

(Causality and mechanism). *Christianity Today,* April 27, 1952.

(Church property grab). *Christianity Today,* September 28, 1962.

(Ethics). *Christianity Today,* September 2, 1966.

(Government and ethics). *Christianity Today,* December 21, 1962.

(Greek views of God). *Christianity Today,* September 10, 1971.

(Liberalism). *Christianity Today,* January 7, 1957.

(Liberalism). *Christianity Today,* March 18, 1957.

(Liberalism). *Christianity Today,* June 18, 1964.

(Malcolm X, Stokely Carmichael, and Eldridge Cleaver). *Christianity Today,* January 16, 1970.

(The order of salvation). *Present Truth,* June 1973; September 1976.

(The problem of evil). *Christianity Today,* May 21, 1971.

(Roman Catholicism). *Christianity Today,* March 27, 1964.

(Scholasticism and the Reformation). *Christianity Today,* November 19, 1965.

(Social engineering). *Christianity Today,* May 11, 1959.

The Crisis of Our Time

Historians have christened the thirteenth century the Age of Faith and termed the eighteenth century the Age of Reason. The twentieth century has been called many things: the Atomic Age, the Age of Inflation, the Age of the Tyrant, the Age of Aquarius. But it deserves one name more than the others: the Age of Irrationalism. Contemporary secular intellectuals are anti-intellectual. Contemporary philosophers are anti-philosophy. Contemporary theologians are anti-theology.

In past centuries secular philosophers have generally believed that knowledge is possible to man. Consequently they expended a great deal of thought and effort trying to justify knowledge. In the twentieth century, however, the optimism of the secular philosophers has all but disappeared. They despair of knowledge.

Like their secular counterparts, the great theologians and doctors of the church taught that knowledge is possible to man. Yet the theologians of the twentieth century have repudiated that belief. They also despair of knowledge. This radical skepticism has filtered down from the philosophers and theologians and penetrated our entire culture, from television to music to literature. *The*

Christian in the twentieth century is confronted with an over-whelming cultural consensus—sometimes stated explicitly, but most often implicitly: Man does not and cannot know anything truly.

What does this have to do with Christianity? Simply this: If man can know nothing truly, man can truly know nothing. We cannot know that the Bible is the Word of God, that Christ died for sin, or that Christ is alive today at the right hand of the Father. Unless knowledge is possible, Christianity is nonsensical, for it claims to be knowledge. What is at stake in the twentieth century is not simply a single doctrine, such as the Virgin Birth, or the existence of hell, as important as those doctrines may be, but the whole of Christianity itself. If knowledge is not possible to man, it is worse than silly to argue points of doctrine—it is insane.

The irrationalism of the present age is so thorough-going and pervasive that even the Remnant—the segment of the professing church that remains faithful—has accepted much of it, frequently without even being aware of what it was accepting. In some circles this irrationalism has become synonymous with piety and humility, and those who oppose it are denounced as rationalists—as though to be logical were a sin. Our contemporary anti-theologians make a contradiction and call it a Mystery. The faithful ask for truth and are given Paradox. If any balk at swallowing the absurdities of the anti-theologians, they are frequently marked as heretics or schismatics who seek to act independently of God.

There is no greater threat facing the true Church of Christ at this moment than the irrationalism that now controls our entire culture. Communism, guilty of tens of millions of murders, including those of millions of Christians, is to be feared, but not nearly so much as the idea that we do not and cannot know the truth. Hedonism, the popular philosophy of America, is not to be feared so much as the belief that logic—that "mere human logic," to use the religious irrationalists' own phrase—is futile. The attacks on truth, on revelation, on the intellect, and on logic are renewed daily. But note well: The misologists—the haters of logic—use logic to demonstrate the futility of using logic. The anti-intellectuals construct intricate intellectual arguments to prove the insufficiency of the intellect. The anti-theologians use the revealed Word of God to show that there can be no revealed Word of God—or that if there could, it would remain impenetrable darkness and Mystery to our finite minds.

Nonsense Has Come

Is it any wonder that the world is grasping at straws—the straws of experientialism, mysticism and drugs? After all, if people are told that the Bible contains insoluble mysteries, then is not a flight into mysticism to be expected? On what grounds can it be condemned? Certainly not on logical grounds or Biblical grounds, if logic is futile and the Bible unintelligible. Moreover, if it cannot be condemned on logical or Biblical grounds, it cannot be condemned at all. If people are going to have a religion of the mysterious, they will not adopt Christianity: They will have a genuine mystery religion. "Those who call for Nonsense," C.S. Lewis once wrote, "will find that it comes." And that is precisely what has happened. The popularity of Eastern mysticism, of drugs, and of religious experience is the logical consequence of the irrationalism of the twentieth century. There can and will be no Christian revival

—and no reconstruction of society—unless and until the irrationalism of the age is totally repudiated by Christians.

The Church Defenseless

Yet how shall they do it? The spokesmen for Christianity have been fatally infected with irrationalism. The seminaries, which annually train thousands of men to teach millions of Christians, are the finishing schools of irrationalism, completing the job begun by the government schools and colleges. Some of the pulpits of the most conservative churches (we are not speaking of the apostate churches) are occupied by graduates of the anti-theological schools. These products of modern anti-theological education, when asked to give a reason for the hope that is in them, can generally respond with only the intellectual analogue of a shrug—a mumble about Mystery. They have not grasped—and therefore cannot teach those for whom they are responsible—the first truth: "And ye shall know the truth." Many, in fact, explicitly deny it, saying that, at best, we possess only "pointers" to the truth, or something "similar" to the truth, a mere analogy. Is the impotence of the Christian Church a puzzle? Is the fascination with pentecostalism and faith healing among members of conservative churches an enigma? Not when one understands the sort of studied nonsense that is purveyed in the name of God in the seminaries.

The Trinity Foundation

The creators of The Trinity Foundation firmly believe that theology is too important to be left to the licensed theologians—the graduates of the schools of theology. They have created The Trinity Foundation for the express purpose of teaching the faithful all that the Scriptures contain—not warmed over, baptized, secular philosophies. Each member of the board of directors of The Trinity Foundation has signed this oath: "I believe that the Bible alone and the Bible in its entirety is the Word of God and, therefore, inerrant in the autographs. I believe that the system of truth presented in the Bible is best summarized in the Westminster Confession of Faith. So help me God."

The ministry of The Trinity Foundation is the presentation of the system of truth taught in Scripture as clearly and as completely as possible. We do not regard obscurity as a virtue, nor confusion as a sign of spirituality. Confusion, like all error, is sin, and teaching that confusion is all that Christians can hope for is doubly sin.

The presentation of the truth of Scripture necessarily involves the rejection of error. The Foundation has exposed and will continue to expose the irrationalism of the twentieth century, whether its current spokesman be an existentialist philosopher or a professed Reformed theologian. We oppose anti-intellectualism, whether it be espoused by a neo-orthodox theologian or a fundamentalist evangelist. We reject misology, whether it be on the lips of a neo-evangelical or those of a Roman Catholic charismatic. To each error we bring the brilliant light of Scripture, proving all things, and holding fast to that which is true.

The Primacy of Theory

The ministry of The Trinity Foundation is not a "practical" ministry. If you are a pastor, we will not enlighten you on how to organize an ecumenical prayer meeting in your community or how to double church attendance in a year. If you are a homemaker, you will have to read elsewhere to find out how to become a total woman. If you are a businessman, we will not tell you how to develop a social conscience. The professing church is drowning in such "practical" advice.

The Trinity Foundation is unapologetically theoretical in its outlook, believing that theory without practice is dead, and that practice without theory is blind. The trouble with the professing church is not primarily in its practice, but in its theory. Christians do not know, and many do not even care to know, the doctrines of Scripture. Doctrine is intellectual, and Christians are generally anti-intellectual. Doctrine is ivory tower philosophy, and they scorn ivory towers. The ivory tower, however, is the control tower of a civilization. It is a fundamental, theoretical mistake of the practical men to think that they can be merely practical, for practice is always the practice of some theory. The relationship between theory and practice is the relationship between cause and effect. If a person believes correct theory, his practice will tend to be correct. The practice of contemporary Christians is immoral because it is the practice of false theories. It is a major theoretical mistake of the practical men to think that they can ignore the ivory towers of the philosophers and theologians as irrelevant to their lives. Every action that the "practical" men take is governed by the thinking that has occurred in some ivory tower—whether that tower be the British Museum, the Academy, a home in Basel, Switzerland, or a tent in Israel.

In Understanding Be Men

It is the first duty of the Christian to understand

correct theory—correct doctrine—and thereby implement correct practice. This order—first theory, then practice—is both logical and Biblical. It is, for example, exhibited in Paul's epistle to the Romans, in which he spends the first eleven chapters expounding theory and the last five discussing practice. The contemporary teachers of Christians have not only reversed the order, they have inverted the Pauline emphasis on theory and practice. The virtually complete failure of the teachers of the professing church to instruct the faithful in correct doctrine is the cause of the misconduct and cultural impotence of Christians. The Church's lack of power is the result of its lack of truth. The *Gospel* is the power of God, not religious experience or personal relationship. The Church has no power because it has abandoned the Gospel, the good news, for a religion of experientialism. Twentieth century American Christians are children carried about by every wind of doctrine, not knowing what they believe, or even if they believe anything for certain.

The chief purpose of The Trinity Foundation is to counteract the irrationalism of the age and to expose the errors of the teachers of the church. Our emphasis—on the Bible as the sole source of truth, on the primacy of the intellect, on the supreme importance of correct doctrine, and on the necessity for systematic and logical thinking—is almost unique in Christendom. To the extent that the church survives—and she will survive and flourish—it will be because of her increasing acceptance of these basic ideas and their logical implications.

We believe that the Trinity Foundation is filling a vacuum in Christendom. We are saying that Christianity is intellectually defensible—that, in fact, it is the only intellectually defensible system of thought. We are saying that

God has made the wisdom of this world—whether that wisdom be called science, religion, philosophy, or common sense—foolishness. We are appealing to all Christians who have not conceded defeat in the intellectual battle with the world to join us in our efforts to raise a standard to which all men of sound mind can repair.

The love of truth, of God's Word, has all but disappeared in our time. We are committed to and pray for a great instauration. But though we may not see this reformation of Christendom in our lifetimes, we believe it is our duty to present the whole counsel of God because Christ has commanded it. The results of our teaching are in God's hands, not ours. Whatever those results, His Word is never taught in vain, but always accomplishes the result that He intended it to accomplish. Professor Gordon H. Clark has stated our view well:

> There have been times in the history of God's people, for example, in the days of Jeremiah, when refreshing grace and widespread revival were not to be expected: the time was one of chastisement. If this twentieth century is of a similar nature, individual Christians here and there can find comfort and strength in a study of God's Word. But if God has decreed happier days for us and if we may expect a world-shaking and genuine spiritual awakening, then it is the author's belief that a zeal for souls, however necessary, is not the sufficient condition. Have there not been devout saints in every age, numerous enough to carry on a revival? Twelve such persons are plenty. What distinguishes the arid ages from the period of the Reformation, when nations were moved as they had not been since Paul preached in Ephesus, Corinth, and Rome, is the latter's fullness of knowledge of God's Word. To echo an early Reformation thought, when the ploughman and the garage attendant

know the Bible as well as the theologian does, and know it better than some contemporary theologians, then the desired awakening shall have already occurred.

In addition to publishing books, of which *Gordon H. Clark: Personal Recollections* is the twenty-seventh, the Foundation publishes a bimonthly newsletter, *The Trinity Review.* Subscriptions to *The Review* are free; please write to the address below to become a subscriber. If you would like further information or would like to join us in our work, please let us know.

The Trinity Foundation is a non-profit foundation tax-exempt under section 501 (c)(3) of the Internal Revenue Code of 1954. You can help us disseminate the Word of God through your tax-deductible contributions to the Foundation.

And we know that the Son of God is come, and hath given us an understanding, that we may know him that is true, and we are in him that is true, in his Son Jesus Christ. This is the true God, and eternal life.

John W. Robbins
President

Intellectual Ammunition

The Trinity Foundation is committed to the reconstruction of philosophy and theology along Biblical lines. We regard God's command to bring all our thoughts into conformity with Christ very seriously, and the books listed below are designed to accomplish that goal. They are written with two subordinate purposes: (1) to demolish all secular claims to knowledge; and (2) to build a system of truth based upon the Bible alone.

Works of Philosophy

Behaviorism and Christianity, Gordon H. Clark $5.95
    Behaviorism *is a critique of both secular and religious behaviorists. It includes chapters on John Watson, Edgar S. Singer Jr., Gilbert Ryle, B.F. Skinner, and Donald MacKay. Clark's refutation of behaviorism and his argument for a Christian doctrine of man are unanswerable.*

A Christian Philosophy of Education, Gordon H. Clark $8.95
    The first edition of this book was published in 1946. It sparked the contemporary interest in Christian schools. Dr. Clark has thoroughly revised and updated it, and it is needed now more than ever. Its chapters include: The Need for a World-View, The Christian World-View, The

Alternative to Christian Theism, Neutrality, Ethics, The Christian Philosophy of Education, Academic Matters, Kindergarten to University. Three appendices are included as well: The Relationship of Public Education to Christianity, A Protestant World-View, and Art and the Gospel.

A Christian View of Men and Things, Gordon H. Clark $8.95
No other book achieves what A Christian View does: the presentation of Christianity as it applies to history, politics, ethics, science, religion, and epistemology. Clark's command of both worldly philosophy and Scripture is evident on every page, and the result is a breathtaking and invigorating challenge to the wisdom of this world.

Clark Speaks From The Grave, Gordon H. Clark $3.95
Dr. Clark chides some of his critics for their failure to defend Christianity competently. Clark Speaks is a stimulating and illuminating discussion of the errors of contemporary apologists.

Education, Christianity, and the State $7.95
J. Gresham Machen
Machen was one of the foremost educators, theologians, and defenders of Christianity in the twentieth century. The author of numerous scholarly books, Machen saw clearly that if Christianity is to survive and flourish, a system of Christian grade schools must be established. This collection of essays captures his thought on education over nearly three decades.

Gordon H. Clark: Personal Recollections, $6.95
John W. Robbins, editor
Friends of Dr. Clark have written their recollections of the man. Contributors include family members, colleagues, students, and friends such as Harold Lindsell, Carl Henry, Ronald Nash, Dwight Zeller, and Mary Crumpacker. The book includes an extensive bibliography of Clark's work.

Logic, Gordon H. Clark $8.95
Written as a textbook for Christian schools, Logic is another unique book from Clark's pen. His presentation of the laws of thought, which must

be followed if Scripture is to be understood correctly, and which are found in Scripture itself, is both clear and thorough. Logic *is an indispensable book for the thinking Christian.*

The Philosophy of Science and Belief in God $5.95
Gordon H. Clark
In opposing the contemporary idolatry of science, Clark analyzes three major aspects of science: the problem of motion, Newtonian science, and modern theories of physics. His conclusion is that science, while it may be useful, is always false; and he demonstrates its falsity in numerous ways. Since science is always false, it can offer no objection to the Bible and Christianity.

Religion, Reason and Revelation, Gordon H. Clark $7.95
One of Clark's apologetical masterpieces, Religion, Reason and Revelation *has been praised for the clarity of its thought and language. It includes chapters on Is Christianity a Religion? Faith and Reason, Inspiration and Language, Revelation and Morality, and God and Evil. It is must reading for all serious Christians.*

Thales to Dewey: A History of Philosophy, paper $11.95
Gordon H. Clark hardback $16.95
This volume is the best one volume history of philosophy in English.

Three Types of Religious Philosophy, Gordon H. Clark $6.95
In this book on apologetics, Clark examines empiricism, rationalism, dogmatism, and contemporary irrationalism, which does not rise to the level of philosophy. He offers a solution to the question, "How can Christianity be defended before the world?"

William James, Gordon H. Clark $2.00
America has not produced many philosophers, but William James has been extremely influential. Clark examines his philosophy of Pragmatism.

Works of Theology

The Atonement, Gordon H. Clark $8.95
This is a major addition to Clark's multi-volume systematic theology. In The Atonement, *Clark discusses the Covenants, the Virgin Birth and Incarnation, federal headship and representation, the relationship between God's sovereignty and justice, and much more. He analyzes traditional views of the Atonement and criticizes them in the light of Scripture alone.*

The Biblical Doctrine of Man, Gordon H. Clark $5.95
Is man soul and body or soul, spirit, and body? What is the image of God? Is Adam's sin imputed to his children? Is evolution true? Are men totally depraved? What is the heart? These are some of the questions discussed and answered from Scripture in this book.

Cornelius Van Til: The Man and The Myth $2.45
John W. Robbins
The actual teachings of this eminent Philadelphia theologian have been obscured by the myths that surround him. This book penetrates those myths and criticizes Van Til's surprisingly unbiblical views of God and the Bible.

Faith and Saving Faith, Gordon H. Clark $6.95
The views of the Roman Catholic church, John Calvin, Thomas Manton, John Owen, Charles Hodge, and B.B. Warfield are discussed in this book. Is the object of faith a person or a proposition? Is faith more than belief? Is belief more than thinking with assent, as Augustine said? In a world chaotic with differing views of faith, Clark clearly explains the Biblical view of faith and saving faith.

God's Hammer: The Bible and Its Critics, Gordon H.
Clark $6.95
The starting point of Christianity, the doctrine on which all other doctrines depend, is "The Bible alone is the Word of God written, and

therefore inerrant in the autographs." Over the centuries the opponents of Christianity, with Satanic shrewdness, have concentrated their attacks on the truthfulness and completeness of the Bible. In the twentieth century the attack is not so much in the fields of history and archaeology as in philosophy. Clark's brilliant defense of the complete truthfulness of the Bible is captured in this collection of eleven major essays.

The Incarnation, Gordon H. Clark $8.95
Who was Christ? The attack on the Incarnation in the nineteenth and twentieth centuries has been vigorous, but the orthodox response has been lame. Clark reconstructs the doctrine of the Incarnation building upon and improving upon the Chalcedonian definition.

In Defense of Theology, Gordon H. Clark $12.95
There are four groups to whom Clark addresses this book: the average Christians who are uninterested in theology, the atheists and agnostics, the religious experientalists, and the serious Christians. The vindication of the knowledge of God against the objections of three of these groups is the first step in theology.

The Johannine Logos, Gordon H. Clark $5.95
Clark analyzes the relationship between Christ, who is the truth, and the Bible. He explains why John used the same word to refer to both Christ and his teaching. Chapters deal with the Prologue to John's Gospel, Logos and Rheemata, Truth, and Saving Faith.

Logical Criticisms of Textual Criticism, Gordon H. Clark $2.95
In this critique of the science of textual criticism, Dr. Clark exposes the fallacious argumentation of the modern textual critics and defends the view that the early Christians knew better than the modern critics which manuscripts of the New Testament were more accurate.

Pat Robertson: A Warning to America, John W. Robbins $6.95
The Protestant Reformation was based on the Biblical principle that the Bible is the only revelation from God, yet a growing political-religious movement, led by Pat Robertson, asserts that God speaks to them directly.

This book addresses the serious issue of religious fanaticism in America by examining the theological and political views of Pat Robertson.

Predestination, Gordon H. Clark $7.95

    Clark thoroughly discusses one of the most controversial and pervasive doctrines of the Bible: that God is, quite literally, Almighty. Free will, the origin of evil, God's omniscience, creation, and the new birth are all presented within a Scriptural framework. The objections of those who do not believe in the Almighty God are considered and refuted. This edition also contains the text of the booklet, Predestination in the Old Testament.

Scripture Twisting in the Seminaries. Part 1: Feminism $5.95
John W. Robbins
    An analysis of the views of three graduates of Westminster Seminary on the role of women in the church.

The Trinity, Gordon H. Clark $8.95

    Apart from the doctrine of Scripture, no teaching of the Bible is more important than the doctrine of God. Clark's defense of the orthodox doctrine of the Trinity is a principal portion of a major new work of Systematic Theology now in progress. There are chapters on the deity of Christ, Augustine, the incomprehensibility of God, Bavinck and Van Til, and the Holy Spirit, among others.

What Do Presbyterians Believe? Gordon H. Clark $7.95

    This classic introduction to Christian doctrine has been republished. It is the best commentary on the Westminster Confession of Faith that has ever been written.

Commentaries on the New Testament

Colossians, Gordon H. Clark $6.95
Ephesians, Gordon H. Clark $8.95

First and Second Thessalonians, Gordon H. Clark $5.95
The Pastoral Epistles (I and II Timothy and Titus) $9.95
    Gordon H. Clark
    All of Clark's commentaries are expository, not technical, and are written for the Christian layman. His purpose is to explain the text clearly and accurately so that the Word of God will be thoroughly known by every Christian. Revivals of Christianity come only through the spread of God's truth. The sound exposition of the Bible, through preaching and through commentaries on Scripture, is the only method of spreading that truth.

The Trinity Review

    The Foundation's bimonthly newsletter, *The Trinity Review*, has been published since 1979 and has carried more than sixty major essays by Gordon H. Clark, J. Gresham Machen, Fyodor Dostoyevsky, Charles Hodge, John Witherspoon, and others. Back issues are available for 40¢ each.

The Trinity Library

We will send you one copy of each of the 30 books listed above for the low price of $150. The regular price of these books is $218. Or you may order the books you want individually on the order blank on the next page. Because some of the books are in short supply, we must reserve the right to substitute others of equal or greater value in The Trinity Library.

Thank you for your attention. We hope to hear from you soon. This special offer expires June 30, 1991.

Order Form

Name _____

Address _____

_____

Please: ☐ add my name to the mailing list for *The Trinity Review* I
understand that there is no charge for the *Review*

☐ accept my tax deductible contribution of $_____
for the work of the Foundation.

☐ send me _____ copies of *Gordon H. Clark: Personal
Recollections*. I enclose as payment $_____.

☐ send me the Trinity Library of 30 books. I enclose $150
as full payment for it.

☐ send me the following books. I enclose full payment
in the amount of $ _____ for them.

_____

_____

_____

_____

_____

_____

_____

Mail to: The Trinity Foundation
Post Office Box 169
Jefferson, MD 21755

Please add $1.00 for postage on orders less than $10. Thank you.
For quantity discounts, please write to the Foundation.